Our Lives in Recovery

A Book for Those Whose Lives Have Been Affected by Incarceration

By Art Lyons

For information on reordering please contact:

Vision Publishing
1115 D Street
Ramona, CA 92065
1-800-9-VISION
www.visionpublishingservices.com

Table of Contents

Preface

What a privilege it is to serve the Lord. If I were to die today, I would have no regrets. I surely can say I have lived a life that has been full of God's adventures in healing and restoration.

At the point of this writing, I have been ministering in correctional facilities for over 30 years. I am thankful that I have had many opportunities to share my spiritual journey with inmates and to encourage them towards faith in Jesus Christ. But better than that, I am thankful that I have been able to hear their stories on how God has changed their lives from addictions to drugs to addictions to Jesus. It is from our collective experience that this book comes about.

No one experiences success in any area of his life without help and encouragement from a multitude of friends. I know that has been true in my life. I would like to thank all of you who have helped me get to this point of ministry. To list you all would be an impossible task. There has been just too many of you for me to count. Yet, I would like to give special thanks to those who have helped this book become a reality:

Dave Chamberlain for your constant encouragement of this project. Eva Chamberlain for the first two edits of this book and helpful suggestions. Diana Hall for her final edits and literary insights. The RPJM Board of Directors who have stuck with me for all these years. The Canyon Community Church Members and Elders who have allowed me to minister inside and outside correctional facilities without restraint. And to all of you who have lifted me up prayerfully and financially. Finally, I would like to thank the Triune God who without Your love and support, I could do nothing.

Yours in Service,

Chaplain Art Lyons

Introduction

Welcome to Re-Entry Prison and Jail Ministry's "Our Lives in Recovery" discipleship course.

This course was developed over twenty-seven years while working with people whose lives have been affected by incarceration or chemical abuse. Over these years, I have observed certain themes and issues that seem to be constant while working with people coming out of an addictive lifestyle. Usually I addressed these key issues in recovery homes because it has been the best environment to work through this material. However, whether you are taking these discipleship classes in a transitional home or in a correctional institution, you should find them helpful.

These classes are based on scriptural principles. It is crucial at this point that you have made a confession of faith in Jesus Christ. You must also have a desire to learn what the Bible says about living a Godly life. If this is true, then God is living in you, and He has given you the ability to do all that will be covered in these classes.

If this is not the case, and you have not given your life to Christ, I invite you to do this now. The Bible tells us that if we confess we are sinners in need of forgiveness, grace, and mercy, we can come to Jesus in prayer and ask for these things. If you are ready now, pray this prayer with me:

Dear God, I acknowledge that I am a sinner in need of Your forgiveness. I have lived my life in my own way and it has brought me nothing but pain and trouble. I ask

You now to come into my life and forgive me of my sins. I ask You to take over my life and teach me Your ways. I thank You now for the forgiveness I am receiving, and I ask You to empower me with the Holy Spirit that I may live a new life in a new way. Amen.

If you have just prayed this prayer in sincere faith, you are now one of God's new children, and I applaud you for your courage. You now will find that God will give you a new ability to follow Him.

Apply yourself diligently to these lessons and do the homework that is suggested for each course. Remember, it took you a long time to get yourself into the situation that brought you to where you are now. So, it will take some time to get totally free from the bondages of chemical abuse and sinful living. These courses are designed to last several weeks and to be applied over a season of time. Be patient and give the Lord time to work in your life through this course. Let me know if this discipleship course has benefited you in any way. You can find my contact information in the back of the book.

May God bless you on your journey to recovery.

Chapter One
Our Emotions and Body Appetites
Part One

Before we were Christians we generally did what we pleased, when we pleased. This is especially true if we have been addicted to drugs or alcohol. Once we give our lives to Christ, the Lord begins to challenge us to bring our body appetites and emotions, what I will refer to as our passions, under His Lordship.

Although we will never get close to controlling ourselves perfectly until the Lord returns, we need to ask ourselves these questions: Who is in control of our passions? Are we ruling our body appetites and emotions or are they ruling us? If we are not in control of them, they will be in control of us. And we will be constantly struggling in the unending cycles of our addictions.

Of course, there will always be inward struggles. In Romans 7:15-25, the Apostle Paul relates to the struggle we all have in wanting to follow Christ but how we are seemingly unable to because of the law of sin that resides in our flesh. The following is what Paul says about this struggle:

> *"For what I am doing, I do not understand. For what I will to do, that I do not practice; but what I hate, that I do. If, then, I do what I will not to do, I agree with*

the law that it is good. But now, it is no longer I who do it, but sin that dwells in me. For I know that in me (that is, in my flesh) nothing good dwells; for to will is present with me, but how to perform what is good I do not find. For the good that I will to do, I do not do; but the evil I will not to do, that I practice. Now if I do what I will not to do, it is no longer I who do it, but sin that dwells in me.

I find then a law, that evil is present with me, the one who wills to do good. For I delight in the law of God according to the inward man. But I see another law in my members, warring against the law of my mind, and bringing me into captivity to the law of sin which is in my members. O wretched man that I am! Who will deliver me from this body of death? I thank God— through Jesus Christ our Lord!

So then, with the mind I myself serve the law of God, but with the flesh the law of sin. "

In this difficult and redundant passage, Paul was trying to communicate that we will battle the flesh in certain areas of our lives until we go to the grave. In this conflict, we need to realize that this struggle is not something for which we should condemn ourselves, but rather we should rejoice in the struggle. It reminds us that we are no longer walking in spiritual darkness, but are now new creations in Christ Jesus as 2nd Corinthians 5:17 tells us below:

> *"Therefore, if anyone is in Christ, he is a new creation; old things have passed away; behold, all things have become new."*

I admit that understanding our spiritual state is difficult at times. It's because we are living in two places as Christians. One place is our true spiritual state and the other is our physical state. One is heavenly; and the other is earthly. As believers, our true spiritual state is a sinless one before God. Yet our true physical state is a corrupted one by the sin nature.

This is a struggle that all believers go through, so how can we reconcile these two worlds?

To explain this dilemma, we need to go back to Chapter Six of Romans. There the Apostle Paul tells us that *technically,* our fleshly passions have been crucified. We need to account our old nature to have been put to death on the cross with Jesus' crucifixion. This sounds like a done deal when we read it, but then we still find ourselves sinning, as Paul admitted he did in Chapter Seven of Romans. The problem is we fail to recognize that when we receive Christ, we are given power by the Holy Spirit to overcome *habitual sin* but not our *sin nature.*

As much as some of us would like to rid ourselves of a particular sin, shortcoming, or bad habit—we have to admit we cannot crucify ourselves. We may be able to drive a nail into our feet, and into one hand, but we are then left upon the cross with hammer in hand and an incomplete job.

So even though we cannot crucify ourselves, we still have to participate in the daily crucifixion of our flesh. How? By drawing close to God. In James 4:8, the Bible tells us that if we will draw close to God, He will draw close to us. In other words, if we are willing to make the effort to do what God says, He will meet us more than halfway.

Although a particular sin may be our life's struggle, we still have to begin to get victory over the outward manifestations of that sin.

Solomon writes in Proverbs 25:28, *"A man who is not in control of his spirit is like a broken down city without any walls."*

We need strong walls of defense to guard against the enemy. If we do not build up our defenses, Satan will constantly be invading our hearts and minds. This book focuses on building around us the defensive walls we need to have to keep the enemy out. Yet, don't forget, as you fortify your defenses, to build into those walls, a very functional gate that allows the Lord entrance to your heart and mind.

In ancient China, around 250 B.C., the Chinese people desired security from the barbaric, invading hoards to the north. To get this protection, they built the

Great Wall of China. This wall is 30 feet high, 18 feet thick, and more than 1,500 miles long! It is the largest man-made structure in the world.

The Chinese goal was to build an absolutely impenetrable defense–too high to climb over, too thick to break down, and too long to go around. But during the first 100 years of the wall's existence, China was successfully invaded three times.

It wasn't the wall's fault. During all three invasions the barbaric hordes never climbed over the wall, they never broke it down, and they never went around it; they simply bribed a gatekeeper and then marched right in through the open gate. The purpose of the wall failed because they neglected to give attention to the integrity of those who guarded the gates. And evidently, they did not learn from their mistakes, because this happened three times.

We are the gatekeepers of our own wall. We decide what enters—the Lord or invading forces.

How is the spiritual integrity of the gates to your heart and mind? Do you have a strong guard protecting the gates to your ears and eyes?

> Our prayer everyday should be, *"Set a guard, O LORD, over my mouth; Keep watch over the door of my lips.* (Psalm 141:3)

Accepting Christ as Savior is the most important step a person can take towards recovery. But this is only the first step. Salvation is more than being saved from the fires of hell. In God's plan of salvation, He also wants to empower us to be saved daily from habitual acts of sin.

Another word for salvation is sanctification. Sanctification means to be set apart and to be made holy. God describes holiness in the Bible as being like Him. That is, desiring the things that He desires. When we accept Christ into our hearts, God sets us apart for Himself. He sanctifies us by imparting His Spirit within us. He gives us eternal life, and He alone makes us holy. However, we also have a responsibility to set ourselves apart for holy living. We are to keep our bodies, spirits, and speech under the Lordship of Jesus Christ.

In the Old Testament, God commands Israel to offer Him animal sacrifices. He tells Israel that these sacrifices and burnt offerings represent the sin of man transferred to the animals that were sacrificed. God told Israel that these sacrifices were a sweet aroma unto him. Why? Because it represented repentance and the willingness to sacrifice or destroy the sinful desires of the flesh.

As mentioned earlier, we will never be able to achieve perfection. That was Jesus' job. He was the perfect sacrifice for man, and He offered Himself in our place. Jesus paid the price for our sin. Christ's sacrifice was sufficient to appease the judgment of God that would normally have fallen on us. Because Christ's sacrifice was accepted in our place, we now have peace with God and God is at peace with us (Romans 8:1).

In the New Testament we are told to become living sacrifices. In Romans 12: 1-2, Paul writes:

"I beseech you therefore, brethren, by

the mercies of God, that you present your bodies a living sacrifice, holy, acceptable to God, which is your reasonable service. And do not be conformed to this world, but be transformed by the renewing of your mind, that you may prove what is that good and acceptable and perfect will of God."

However, there is a problem with living sacrifices. They tend to crawl off the altar.

I have met many of these wayward "living sacrifices." You too may have experienced heartache from seeing Christian loved ones walk away from God. Yet, we can find comfort in this: God will put His "rubber band" of love around those who really want to follow Christ.

What do I mean by this?

When a Christian allows his sinful passions to lead him away from Christ, this backslidden person experiences Godly tension. This tension will increase until he lets go of his sinful quest. I have met many people in jail, prison, and recovery homes who have finally given in to that "rubber band" of God's love. And know this—if you are currently resisting God's calling in your life—the further you stretch away, the more problems you will have to resolve when you return back to God.

If we want to experience a greater portion of God's blessing in our lives, we need to bring our passions under the Lordship of Christ. This means we must start walking in holiness.

So what is holiness? The Bible is what the Lord uses

to define holiness. The Bible also defines what is considered by God to be sinful behavior. By reading the scriptures and observing the life of Christ, we can learn what it means to walk in holiness.

Among the many sins of passion, the Bible indicates to us that fornication (sexual sin) is the most destructive. In 1st Thessalonians 4:1-8, we are encouraged to possess our vessels (bodies) in sanctification by letting the Holy Spirit possess us. We read there:

> *"Finally then, brethren, we urge and exhort in the Lord Jesus that you should abound more and more, just as you received from us how you ought to walk and to please God; for you know what commandments we gave you through the Lord Jesus.*
>
> *For this is the will of God, your sanctification: that you should abstain from sexual immorality; that each of you should know how to possess his own vessel in sanctification and honor, not in passion of lust, like the Gentiles who do not know God; that no one should take advantage of and defraud his brother in this matter, because the Lord is the avenger of all such, as we also forewarned you and testified. For God did not call us to uncleanness, but in holiness. Therefore he who rejects this does not reject man, but God, who has also given us His Holy Spirit."*

The Bible tells us that when we join ourselves to sin we actually involve Christ. Not that we are causing Christ to sin, but the Holy Spirit within us is being grieved when we sin. This is mentioned in Ephesians 4:30-32:

> *"And do not grieve the Holy Spirit of God, by whom you were sealed for the day of redemption. Let all bitterness, wrath, anger, clamor, and evil speaking be put away from you, with all malice. And be kind to one another, tenderhearted, forgiving one another, even as God in Christ forgave you."*

1st Corinthians 6:15-20 says:

> *"Do you not know that your bodies are members of Christ? Shall I then take the members of Christ and make them members of a harlot? Certainly not! Or do you not know that he who is joined to a harlot is one body with her? For 'the two,' He says, 'shall become one flesh.' But he who is joined to the Lord is one spirit with Him.*
> *Flee sexual immorality. Every sin that a man does is outside the body, but he who commits sexual immorality sins against his own body. Or do you not know that your body is the temple of the Holy Spirit who is in you, whom you have from God, and you*

are not your own? For you were bought at a price; therefore glorify God in your body and in your spirit, which are God's."

Here we are instructed to view our bodies as temples of God's Spirit. The Bible teaches us that in every sin a believer commits, two things are happening. God is there with us, and the Holy Spirit is being grieved within us. Hopefully, this spiritual reality will help us think twice before we decide to commit sinful acts as believers.

Homework

Pray this prayer or one like it before you start reading this book or the Bible for the next ten days.

Dear Lord,

I ask you to fill me with a greater presence and awareness of your Holy Spirit. I realize that without your help I cannot live the way you want me to. I believe that you can give me the special ability I need to practically follow the Biblical principles that are discussed in this book and more importantly in the Bible. I thank you right now for doing this. Amen.

<u>Notes</u>

Chapter Two
Our Emotions and Body Appetites
Part Two

In 2nd Peter 1:1-11, the Apostle Peter teaches us three things. First, he teaches us that God has given believers in Christ all that we need to live Godly lives (v. 1-4). Secondly, Peter tells us that we have a responsibility to participate in the process (v. 5-7). Thirdly, Peter exhorts us that there are benefits for participation and consequences if we don't participate (v. 8-11). Stop and read 2nd Peter 1-11 before you continue this study.

We have a responsibility to maintain our daily sanctification by adding to our faith the following seven attributes:

1. **Virtue:** A passion for moral excellence or a strong desire to do what is right.
2. **Knowledge:** Used here in the context of studying and learning of God's Word.
3. **Self-control:** Especially of one's passions (such as in our study) our body appetites and emotions.
4. **Perseverance:** Learning to be diligent or "hanging-in there for the long haul."
5. **Godliness:** Imitating Godly character, living as Jesus did.

6. **Kindness:** Being considerate to those around us, blessing people in word and deed.
7. **Love:** Exercising agape love, loving people without strings attached.

The key benefit mentioned here is that we will never stumble or backslide away from God if we apply to our faith the attributes that Peter has listed above. This is so important to realize for those who are currently incarcerated. It is well documented, that over half of the people who have ever been incarcerated will return to prison or jail within three years of release. Many of these men and women had turned their lives over to Christ when they were previously arrested. So why are they back in prison or jail? Simply because they stopped adding to their faith the attributes that Peter listed. Peter goes on to describe the benefits of adding these attributes to our faith and the result if we do not:

"For if these things are yours and abound, you will be neither barren nor unfruitful in the knowledge of our Lord Jesus Christ. For he who lacks these things is shortsighted, even to blindness, and has forgotten that he was cleansed from his old sins. Therefore, brethren, be even more diligent to make your call and election sure, for if you do these things you will never stumble; for so an entrance will be supplied

to you abundantly into the everlasting kingdom of our Lord and Savior Jesus Christ."

The key that unlocks the door to victorious living in Christ is found in Galatians 5:16, where Paul tells us:

"I say then: Walk in the Spirit, and you shall not fulfill the lust of the flesh."

The Bible makes it clear that there is a battle going on between our spirit and our flesh.

Let's read now the rest of the passage in Galatians, to verse 27:

"For the flesh lusts against the Spirit, and the Spirit against the flesh; and these are contrary to one another, so that you do not do the things that you wish. But if you are led by the Spirit, you are not under the law.

Now the works of the flesh are evident, which are: adultery, fornication, uncleanness, lewdness, idolatry, sorcery, hatred, contentions, jealousies, outbursts of wrath, selfish ambitions, dissensions, heresies, envy, murders, drunkenness, revelries, and the like; of which I tell you beforehand, just as I also told you in time past, that those who practice such things will not inherit the kingdom of God.

But the fruit of the Spirit is love, joy, peace, longsuffering, kindness, goodness, faithfulness, gentleness, self-control. Against such there is no law. And those who are Christ's have crucified the flesh with its passions and desires. If we live in the Spirit, let us also walk in the Spirit. Let us not become conceited, provoking one another, envying one another."

What you just read is really important, especially if you are currently incarcerated or concerned about a habit that will get you arrested. The Bible tells us that if you give your life to Christ, and ask Him to empower you with the Holy Spirit's Fruit, there are some laws you will never break again. Think about it. You cannot be arrested for having too much love, joy, peace, longsuffering, kindness, goodness, faithfulness, gentleness, or self-control.

There is a story told attributed to an American Indian pastor that illustrates these scriptures well. He said the spirit and the flesh are like having two dogs living inside of us – a white dog and a black dog. The white dog represents our spirit; the black dog represents our flesh. These two dogs are constantly fighting. Although they won't ultimately destroy one another, one will always be beating up and dominating the other. We decide which one is dominating by whom we feed and by whom we starve. It's just that simple.

So how do we walk in the spirit and not in the flesh? We do this by living in a spiritual manner; by allowing God to develop the fruit of the Spirit in our lives, or simply yielding our will to God's will.

The Apostle Paul listed many of the changes that should take place in our lives by the power of God in Ephesians 4:17-32. Read through this passage and make note of the various sins that come from our passions. Identify the "put on's" and the "put off's." As you do this, ask yourself, how many different areas of sin can I come up with? Which ones do I need to work on?

"This I say, therefore, and testify in the Lord, that you should no longer walk as the rest of the Gentiles (unbelievers) walk, in the futility of their mind, having their understanding darkened, being alienated from the life of God, because of the ignorance that is in them, because of the blindness of their heart; who, being past feeling, have given themselves over to lewdness, to work all uncleanness with greediness.

But you have not so learned Christ, if indeed you have heard Him and have been taught by Him, as the truth is in Jesus: that you put off, concerning your former conduct, the old man which grows corrupt according to the deceitful lusts, and be renewed in the spirit of your mind, and that you put on the new man which was created according to God, in true righteousness and holiness.

Therefore, putting away lying, let each one of you speak truth with his neighbor, for we are members of one another. 'Be angry, and do not sin': do not let the sun go down on your wrath, nor give place to the devil. Let him who stole steal no longer, but rather let him labor, working with his hands what is good, that he may have something to give him who has need. Let no corrupt word proceed out of your mouth, but what is good for necessary edification, that it may impart grace to the hearers. And do not grieve the Holy Spirit of God, by whom you were sealed for the day of redemption. Let all bitterness, wrath, anger, clamor, and evil speaking be put away from you, with all malice. And be kind to one another, tenderhearted, forgiving one another, even as God in Christ forgave you."

Another aspect of walking in the Spirit, and perhaps the first step to take, is developing a consistent prayer life.

Ephesians 6:18 tells us we should be:

"Praying always with all prayer and supplication in the Spirit, being watchful to this end with all perseverance and supplication for all the saints."

In 1ˢᵗ Thessalonians 5:17, Paul says we should

pray without ceasing. And in Romans 12:11-12 he writes that we should be:

> *"Not lagging in diligence, fervent in spirit, serving the Lord; rejoicing in hope, patient in tribulation, continuing steadfastly in prayer; distributing to the needs of the saints, given to hospitality."*

In the Greek (the original language in which the New Testament was written), the words for "praying continually" was described as a persistent cough, like when you have a tickle in your throat and can't keep from coughing. In other words, we should be offering prayers throughout the day and night for our needs, and the needs of others who come to mind.

Furthermore, we can walk in the spirit by applying the teaching found in Ephesians 5:17-21:

> *"Therefore do not be unwise, but understand what the will of the Lord is. And do not be drunk with wine, in which is dissipation (over-indulgence); but be filled with the Spirit, speaking to one another in psalms and hymns and spiritual songs, singing and making melody in your heart to the Lord, giving thanks always for all things to God the Father in the name of our Lord Jesus Christ, submitting to one another in the fear of God."*

Colossians 3:12-17 tells us:

"Therefore, as the elect of God, holy and beloved, put on tender mercies, kindness, humility, meekness, longsuffering; bearing with one another, and forgiving one another, if anyone has a complaint against another; even as Christ forgave you, so you also must do. But above all these things put on love, which is the bond of perfection. And let the peace of God rule in your hearts, to which also you were called in one body; and be thankful. Let the word of Christ dwell in you richly in all wisdom, teaching and admonishing one another in psalms and hymns and spiritual songs, singing with grace in your hearts to the Lord. And whatever you do in word or deed, do all in the name of the Lord Jesus, giving thanks to God the Father through Him."

These passages of scripture focus on building peace and harmony with our family in Christ. They encourage us to learn how to worship God together. We cannot walk in the Spirit if we are not in fellowship with our Christian brethren and our God. We read throughout the book of 1st John that if we do not want to spend time with God and with our family in Christ, we are not walking in the light (Spirit) but are walking in darkness (the works of the flesh).

You may be thinking, *Ok, I can see in the Bible where it specifically talks about how it's wrong to have sex outside of marriage and to speak with profanity, but what about things like smoking or drinking coffee, or other things that the Bible does not specifically address?*

I believe the Bible addresses all issues, even if they are not that "black and white" in the Bible. For example, I am often asked by Christians who smoke whether their smoking will send them to hell. My response is, "No." It may get you to heaven faster, but smoking will not send you to hell. However, is smoking a sin? "Yes, I believe so."

The Apostle Paul addressed this subject in 1st Corinthians 6:12 where he wrote:

> *"All things are lawful but not all things are expedient"* (or edify) and in 10:23-24, he wrote, *"All things are lawful, but I will not be brought under the power of any."*

In context, Paul was addressing several questions that the Corinthian believers were asking. These questions were: 1) Could Christians buy and eat meat that was sacrificed to idols? And, 2) Should believers attend the feasts that were put on by pagan friends? Some of the believers in the Corinthian Church had a problem doing these things while others felt they had liberty to do them.

In Paul's response, he was not saying Christians could do anything they want. Certainly, we must try to live our lives by what is taught in the Bible, but where scripture is silent; these rules in 1st Corinthians apply.

In other words, we have liberty in the gray areas if we don't offend our brothers and sisters with our liberty– and this "liberty" does not control us. That is why smoking or any substance or activity that can control us– is potentially sinful.

Paul goes on to write in Romans 14:22b:

> *"Happy is he who does not condemn himself in what he approves."*

Or be completely convinced in your own conscience that your behavior is right before the Lord, before letting your emotions and body appetites express themselves.

One of the many observances I have made in reading the Bible is that God always gives us what we want. If we want to be a mature Christian, with all the benefits, we will become one. On the other hand, if we don't want Christ in our lives, we get that too. It all has to do with what we pursue and how hard we pursue it!

Homework

Write down five different disciplines you can practice to keep yourself walking in the Spirit daily. List Bible references for these examples. Return this list to the instructor of this class before the next lesson. If possible, also make a copy of this page for your own reference.

1._____

2._____

3._____

4._____

5._____

<u>Notes</u>

Chapter Three
Restoring Our Family Relationships

The results of a life spent on alcohol and drugs, or in prison, will always put a tremendous strain on relationships. This is especially true in the relationships between the abuser and their family members. In fact, most if not all relational bridges have been burned by the time the offenders reach the end of their own strength and decide to turn their lives over to God.

God created man to be part of a family unit. We function best in a common social environment. Bloodline in the Old Testament was very important. Knowing one's ancestral history and passing down family inheritances was emphasized.

Unfortunately, if a person has come from a long line of drug and alcohol abusers, he may not even know the history of his bloodline past two generations. Divorce, criminal activity, and other embarrassments that accompany severe chemical abuse can cause most parents and grandparents to avoid talking about their painful pasts. In turn, quality character traits, family inheritances, and prestige have ceased to be passed down to the next generation. What is passed down however, are the weaknesses of one's heritage.

If this rings true for you or someone you know, do not be surprised that you have had similar addictions and character deficiencies passed down to you.

In fact, the Bible speaks of this in Exodus 34:5-7 where it tells us we will inherit the blessings and the weaknesses from our families:

> *"Now the LORD descended in the cloud and stood with him there, and proclaimed the name of the LORD. And the LORD passed before him and proclaimed, "The LORD, the LORD God, merciful and gracious, longsuffering, and abounding in goodness and truth, keeping mercy for thousands, forgiving iniquity and transgression and sin, by no means clearing the guilty, visiting the iniquity of the fathers upon the children and the children's children to the third and the fourth generation."*

Although these repercussions of our parents' sin may affect us greatly, and our own life of living foolishly will bring devastation to us, there is good news. The curse can be stopped. Foolish living can be turned into a blessing when we repent of our sins and accept Jesus into our lives.

In the Old Testament in Jeremiah 18:1-10, the Bible tells us that the desire of God's heart is to deliver us from inherited curses:

> *"The word which came to Jeremiah from the LORD, saying: 'Arise and go down to the potter's house, and there I will cause*

you to hear My words.' Then I went down to the potter's house, and there he was, making something at the wheel. And the vessel that he made of clay was marred in the hand of the potter; so he made it again into another vessel, as it seemed good to the potter to make.

Then the word of the LORD came to me, saying: 'O house of Israel, can I not do with you as this potter?' says the LORD. 'Look, as the clay is in the potter's hand, so are you in My hand, O house of Israel! The instant I speak concerning a nation and concerning a kingdom, to pluck up, to pull down, and to destroy it, if that nation against whom I have spoken turns from its evil, I will relent of the disaster that I thought to bring upon it. And the instant I speak concerning a nation and concerning a kingdom, to build and to plant it, if it does evil in My sight so that it does not obey My voice, then I will relent concerning the good with which I said I would benefit it.'"

God declares here that repentance from evil will bring instantaneous results of blessings from the Lord. This was God's remedy long before A.A.'s 12-step plan to recovery was thought up. The Bible has taught us from the beginning of time that true repentance of our sins always brings saving grace.

In the New Testament we see John the Baptist's

ministry was a ministry of repentance with the promise of reconciliation between fathers and their sons (Luke 1:16-17). Once we repent, God will begin to bring reconciliation between family members. Take note here, that John's ministry of repentance preceded Christ's ministry of salvation. Repentance always precedes reconciliation.

The Bible tells us in 2nd Corinthians 5:17-20 that when we become saved, we are born again spiritually. We actually become brand new creatures and our old nature passes away. This new creation is God's Spirit living within us, empowering us to live a Christian life:

> *"Therefore, if anyone is in Christ, he is a new creation; old things have passed away; behold, all things have become new. Now all things are of God, who has reconciled us to Himself through Jesus Christ, and has given us the ministry of reconciliation, that is, that God was in Christ reconciling the world to Himself, not imputing their trespasses to them, and has committed to us the word of reconciliation.*
>
> *Now then, we are ambassadors for Christ, as though God were pleading through us: we implore you on Christ's behalf, be reconciled to God. For He made Him who knew no sin to be sin for us, that we might become the righteousness of God in Him."*

When we become saved, God imparts unto us a ministry of reconciliation. This ministry of reconciliation helps us to restore and rebuild relationships that have been broken from our past sinful behavior, and it is also given to us to help others reconcile their lives to God.

In Romans 8:28 we are promised that God is able to turn all our past sins and mistakes into something good. This includes broken and messed-up relationships:

> *"And we know that all things work together for good to those who love God, to those who are the called according to His purpose."*

This good news should give us hope that family relationships that have been damaged can be restored.

However, even after true repentance and salvation has taken place, reconciliation is not always easy. The past sins of the offender have most likely hurt the family members deeply, and their reactions toward the offender have most likely hurt him. This cycle of pain cannot be broken until two things happen. First, the offender starts the process of repentance visibly. Secondly, family members and friends are willing to take steps towards forgiveness. Just as repentance is the forerunner to salvation, so is forgiveness the forerunner to restoring broken relationships.

The Bible teaches us there are two different types of forgiveness, or two ways forgiveness is administered. The first type of forgiveness, which I will call *"restorative forgiveness"* we will cover now.

Restorative forgiveness is the most desirable. Simply put, the offender repents, we forgive them and restore them to relationship with us.

Jesus emphasized this type of forgiveness in Luke 17:1-4:

> *"Then He said to the disciples, 'It is impossible that no offenses should come, but woe to him through whom they do come! It would be better for him if a millstone were hung around his neck, and he were thrown into the sea, than that he should offend one of these little ones. Take heed to yourselves. If your brother sins against you, rebuke him; and if he repents, forgive him. And if he sins against you seven times in a day, and seven times in a day returns to you, saying, 'I repent,' you shall forgive him.'"*

The importance of restorative forgiveness should not be trivialized. If God expects us to repent of our sins before He will forgive us and grant us restoration with Him, why wouldn't we think He expects the same type of repentance between others and us?

If this is true, we should not be confused and alarmed over our sense of mistrust with the offender if they have not displayed a true repentant behavior. This is the natural human response unless true repentance has taken place. However, if someone has come to us and asks for forgiveness, we must take seriously Jesus' words in Luke 17, even if emotionally we may not be ready to accept an apology.

Now it is true that even though an offender asks for forgiveness, they may not really be sorry for what they have done. The offender may only be demonstrating worldly sorrow—sorrow that they got caught. Sorrow that their self-seeking lifestyle has been inconvenienced by incarceration or homelessness. This is not Godly sorrow.

So how do we know when there is true repentance? The Bible goes on to illustrate that there should be *evidence* of the fruit of repentance to validate one's true heart attitude.

I would like to offer you a recipe that makes up true repentance. The ingredients are confession of sins, restitution, and a change of behavior.

Godly sorrow is evidenced by true repentance, which always is confirmed with visible evidence. This may be shown by voluntary restitution that the Spirit of God will initiate in a repentant person's heart. In the Old Testament God required a thief to restore 120% and sometimes 600% of what he had stolen to make restitution (Exodus 22:1-4, Leviticus 6:4-5).

As New Testament Christians, we are not obligated to follow the Old Testament law, but we are to look for what the Spirit of God was saying through the Law. With that reasoning, I believe that the Holy Spirit will give a repentant person the desire to replace what he has stolen if at all possible. I would say that if you have experienced an offender trying to restore even just half of what he has taken, you can be sure that you have met a repentant person!

John the Baptist also commented on the necessity of producing the fruit of repentance in Luke 3:3-8. There he teaches the evidence of a repentant person is proven by a changed lifestyle. Restitution is further supported in the Bible in the repentance of Zacchaeus in Luke 19:2-10.

In Matthew 18:21-22, we read that Peter asked Jesus:

> *"Lord, how often shall my brother sin against me, and I forgive him? Up to seven times?" Jesus said to him, "I do not say to you, up to seven times, but up to seventy times seven."*

Jesus encourages us to forgive a truly repentant person of the same sin up to 490 times, or as often as he is truly repentant.

We have to watch over our own hearts when we have been offended. We may choose not to forgive a truly repentant person because we have been hurt too many times in the past. This is especially true if that person has spent a lifetime in addiction to chemicals or other activity that has kept them inside correctional institutions for years. Yet, Jesus encourages us to keep our hearts soft towards all people and all offences. It may take several attempts for the offender to truly repent and show fruit of repentance. In Matthew 18, Jesus was trying to communicate to us, that if we do not extend forgiveness to a repentant person, it is sin on our part not to forgive them.

So am I saying the Bible teaches us that we are only obligated to forgive someone when they have repented with concrete evidence supporting their repentance?

Not necessarily.

As I mentioned before, there are two ways that we can forgive. The second way forgiveness can be administered is not centered on restoring but on releasing.

In this scenario, the offender chooses not to repent or can't repent because of death or disability. Under these conditions there will be an emotional hurt left unresolved in the offended. This hurt, that seemingly cannot be fixed or reconciled, can only be healed by God's grace in our lives.

In such cases, if we do not release and forgive the emotional hurt in our own heart, we may find ourselves carrying the pain of unresolved forgiveness. If this continues, we will forever be trapped by resentment and bitterness.

So what can we do? Why would God expect us to offer forgiveness to unrepentant people in our lives? Because, He expects us to forgive as we have been forgiven. Just as He forgives us of our continual offences towards Him and others, we need to forgive every offender in our lives. We need to be thankful for His continual forgiveness to us and to others.

However, let's be honest about who has offended

whom first. Often, when we are working through forgiveness issues between family and friends of incarcerated people, there are usually no real innocent parties. We need to be honest with ourselves concerning our lack of maturity that may have added to the offenses of someone incarcerated.

If we have not been parented well, we probably have not parented our children well. If we have not had good role models of marriage, we probably will not have treated our spouses well. If we have not experienced mature relationships with friends and family members, we probably have reacted immaturely toward others.

We may be as much at fault for the misbehavior of others, or even more at fault than they are. For reconciliation and restorative forgiveness to take place, someone has to be willing to "stop the cycle of beating."

A friend of mine illustrated this by a saying in his home, "Someone has to take a hit and not hit back."

This came from observing his children in the back of the car, arguing with each other. Occasionally his children's disagreements would end up in physical aggression. Each time one would punch the other; the other would retaliate with a hit. This would continue until someone would make the decision to take a hit, and not hit back.

Guess what? Jesus took the hit for us.

Jesus even taught us to go further than that.

In 1st Peter 2:19-25 we read:

"For it is commendable if a man bears

up under the pain of unjust suffering because he is conscious of God. But how is it to your credit if you receive a beating for doing wrong and endure it? But if you suffer for doing good and you endure it, this is commendable before God. To this you were called, because Christ suffered for you, leaving you an example, that you should follow in His steps. 'He committed no sin, and no deceit was found in His mouth.' When they hurled their insults at Him, He did not retaliate; when He suffered, He made no threats. Instead, He entrusted Himself to Him who judges justly. He himself bore our sins in His body on the tree, so that we might die to sins and live for righteousness; by His wounds you have been healed. For you were like sheep going astray, but now you have returned to the Shepherd and Overseer of your souls."

Don't pat yourself on the back for taking suffering you deserve. Pat yourself on the back for having a good attitude while enduring suffering that you did not deserve.

Jesus even wants us to be the initiators of forgiveness. In Matthew 5:23-24 we read:

"Therefore if you bring your gift to the altar, and there remember that your brother

has something against you, leave your gift there before the altar, and go your way. First be reconciled to your brother, and then come and offer your gift."

If we want to win favor with God, we must first forgive those who have offended us. Jesus told us that if we want to be blessed by God we first need to make sure that no one has outstanding offences against us. Only after we have tried to mend these relationships are we in the right standing with God to receive His favor. Jesus talked about how it was important that we take the log out of our own eye first, so we could see to remove the speck in another's eye.

Jesus went even further to say that we are to bless our enemies and speak well of them. If we are commanded to do this to our enemies, then shouldn't we do that much more for our unrepentant loved ones?

In the previous chapter (Our Emotions and Body Appetites), I listed the seven attributes that the Apostle Peter exhorted us to add to our faith (2nd Peter 1:5-7). The last two of those attributes listed were kindness and love. Jesus taught continuously throughout the Gospels that we should be kind and loving, even unto our enemies. In Jesus' time, some historians teach that women would carry pottery on their heads that held hot coals inside. Just like getting water bottles delivered to our homes today, these women went to different homes delivering coals to renew the fires inside. Jesus wants us to offer our enemy service, rather than to see him shiver from lack of heat in his home.

Does that mean we hand unrepentant people our checkbook to do what they want with it? Being kind and loving does not mean we should foolishly trust those with our resources who have not yet come to repentance. The Bible teaches that we are to be good managers of all that God has given us. If we fail to do so, Jesus tells us our portion will be taken from us.

So how do we relate to those who have offended us and have not repented? We are to be kind to them, love them as much as we are able, and release them over to God for accountability.

This type of releasing is illustrated in Romans 12:14-21 where we read:

> "Bless those who persecute you; bless and do not curse. Rejoice with those who rejoice, and weep with those who weep. Be of the same mind toward one another. Do not set your mind on high things, but associate with the humble. Do not be wise in your own opinion.
>
> Repay no one evil for evil. Have regard for good things in the sight of all men. If it is possible, as much as depends on you, live peaceably with all men. Beloved, do not avenge yourselves, but rather give place to wrath; for it is written, 'Vengeance is Mine, I will repay,' says the Lord. Therefore 'If your enemy is hungry, feed him; If he is thirsty, give him a drink;

For in so doing you will heap coals of fire on his head.' Do not be overcome by evil, but overcome evil with good."

We are told not to take revenge on an individual, but to bless them and leave any judgmental consequences for their sin for God to deal with justly. The book of Hebrews tells us *"The goodness of God leads us to repentance."* God will often use the kindness we demonstrate to those who do not like us to break the hardness of their hearts.

Now you may not be having a problem with bitterness or wanting to get even with the person who has offended you. In fact, you may be experiencing what one person mentioned to me while I was teaching a "Family Coping Strategies" workshop. That day, one of the attendees said, "You know, Chaplain Art, love and forgiveness is not the same thing. I love this person incarcerated in my life right now—but it's really hard to forgive them." Truly spoken. We can love and not forgive as well as forgive but not show love. We need to do both as much as is in our ability to do so.

I believe this type of forgiveness (or releasing) will always leave a void in the relationship. Trust cannot really ever be reinstated until the offender truly repents. Release, however, will produce peace in our lives between the offender, God, and us.

Still another problem in reconciling with family members is that there are demonic spiritual forces that are working against the reconciliation of you and your family. Some family members may even tell you that they liked you better before you were saved. They may even try to get you to return to drinking and drugging. Be patient. It will probably take a year or more of growing up in Christ before some family members will trust you again. And be prepared, some may never accept you, your new faith, or like the new person you have become. If this is true for you, remember what Matthew 10:34-39 tells us:

> *"Do not think that I came to bring peace on earth. I did not come to bring peace but a sword. For I have come to 'set a man against his father, a daughter against her mother, and a daughter-in-law against her mother-in-law'; and 'a man's enemies will be those of his own household.' <u>He who loves father or mother more than Me is not worthy of Me.</u> And he who loves son or daughter more than Me is not worthy of Me. And he who does not take his cross and follow after Me is not worthy of Me. He who finds his life will lose it, and he who loses his life for My sake will find it."*

God wants to promote a greater peace in our lives, and He will do it. We must always put Him first (underlined in verse 37 above) and keep Him there. Remember, Jesus promises us a blessing if we are persecuted for <u>righteousness' sake</u> (Matthew 5:10-12), not for being obnoxious!

We also need to be careful that we don't let our newfound piety get in the way of restoring relationships with our family. We must not present our Christianity in a way that makes us look better than our family now that we are saved. Another way that this has been said is, "Don't be so heavenly minded that you're no earthly good." Remember where you came from and how you got to where you are now. You are a sinner too—you're just walking in repentance.

1st Corinthians 4:7 warns us about this:

> *"For who makes you differ from another? And what do you have that you did not receive? Now if you did indeed receive it, why do you boast as if you had not received it?"*

You may now be seeing for the first time the sins and failures of your family in the light of the Bible. If we want to rebuild broken family relationships, we need to guard ourselves from becoming like the Pharisees, which were considered the holy people of Jesus' day. Jesus rebuked the Pharisees because they became self-righteous as we see in Mark 7:9-13:

> *"And he said to them: "You have a fine way of setting aside the commands of God in order to observe your own traditions! For Moses said, 'Honor your father and your mother,' and, 'Anyone who curses his father*

or mother must be put to death.' But you say that if a man says to his father or mother: 'Whatever help you might otherwise have received from me is Corban' (that is, a gift devoted to God), then you no longer let him do anything for his father or mother. Thus you nullify the word of God by your tradition that you have handed down. And you do many things like that."(NIV)

The Pharisees, in the name of religion, would dedicate everything they owned as "devoted to God," so it could not be given to their parents or the poor. In other words, they made their religion more important than their relationships.

While ministering to God is our first priority, our family is our second most important ministry. We read in 1st Timothy 5:8:

"But if anyone does not provide for his own, and especially for those of his household, he has denied the faith and is worse than an unbeliever."

Ephesians talks about how relationships between family members should be governed by cherishing and honoring one another (Ephesians 5:22-6:4). As God leads family members to reconcile, He will begin to re-establish order and respect.

Many men have a distorted view of what it means to

be the head of the household. Many of us have led by dominating other members of the family, forcing those around us to submit to our desires. Later in this series, we will be looking at God's purposes behind submission. For now, we will briefly touch on right relating with family members.

To wives, the apostle Paul writes in Ephesians 5:22-24:

"Wives, submit to your own husbands, as to the Lord. For the husband is head of the wife, as also Christ is head of the church; and He is the Savior of the body. Therefore, just as the church is subject to Christ, so let the wives be to their own husbands in everything."

To husbands, Paul writes in Ephesians 5:25-33:

"Husbands, love your wives, just as Christ also loved the church and gave Himself for her, that He might sanctify and cleanse her with the washing of water by the word, that He might present her to Himself a glorious church, not having spot or wrinkle or any such thing, but that she should be holy and without blemish. So husbands ought to love their own wives as their own bodies; he who loves his wife loves himself. For no one ever hated his own flesh, but

nourishes and cherishes it, just as the Lord does the church. For we are members of His body, of His flesh and of His bones. "For this reason a man shall leave his father and mother and be joined to his wife, and the two shall become one flesh." This is a great mystery, but I speak concerning Christ and the church. Nevertheless let each one of you in particular so love his own wife as himself, and let the wife see that she respects her husband."

To children, Paul wrote in Ephesians 6:1-4:

"Children, obey your parents in the Lord, for this is right. "Honor your father and mother," which is the first command- ment with promise: "that it may be well with you and you may live long on the earth." And you, fathers, do not provoke your children to wrath, but bring them up in the training and admonition of the Lord."

This topic of submission may be causing you some anxiety. If you are a spouse or child of a chemical-dependent person, this is understandable. However, I want to assure you that God's plan in submitting to others was not for the purpose of instituting some tyrannical government over you.

God has created men, women, and children equally as found in Galatians 3:28:

"There is neither Jew nor Greek, there is neither slave nor free, there is neither male nor female; for you are all one in Christ Jesus."

Although God has created men and women equally, the man has more accountability to God. Let me explain submission in the context of the mystery of the Trinity.

True Christianity has always held to the doctrine of the Triune God: God the Father, God the Son, and God the Holy Spirit. One God expressed in three persons. They are all equal but all have different functions in the Trinity. So it is with the family. Husbands, wives, and children are all equal persons in the eyes of God, but all have different functions. The purpose of submission is to regulate order, not to give power to one person to rule over another.

Before we were Christians, we lived our lives in a self-centered manner. Years of bad habits have developed selfish behavior that will take some time to correct, but this can be achieved. Changes come, but often they seem to come too slowly. I compare it to watching our fingernails grow, or watching our hair grow in the mirror. One can see the progress in a week or two, but not at the moment we want to see it happen. Be patient, and you will grow in Christ too.

Homework

1. Write down any names of family members you have offended.

   _____

   _____

   _____

   _____

   _____

2. Pray over this list and ask God to show you what you could do to reconcile any offenses. Write down what you could do in each case.

   _____

   _____

   _____

   _____

   _____

3. Set a target date to accomplish your goals in reconciliation with all of the people on your list.

4. Share these goals with someone you can trust who will encourage you to meet your deadlines.

5. Have the person you shared these goals with contact the instructor, and acknowledge that you have indeed met with him/her to share your goals.

Notes

Chapter Four
Establishing Our Church Family

The focus of this study is to talk about the support system that God has set up to bring us into Christian maturity. This support system is called the Church (the Body of Christ).

We need to commit ourselves to the Body of Christ locally. We need to make ourselves accountable to elders and youngsters in the faith. We need to be committed and submitted to one another. Give your heart, body, soul, and spirit to your present church. If you can't learn to do this now, no matter what living environment you are currently in (whether it is in prison or in a recovery home), you'll never be able to do it later.

The Bible teaches that we are to live our Christian lives with a commitment to God and the church. We are not to look to any man except Jesus Christ to be the ultimate authority in our lives. Yet, God uses Godly men and women to teach and instruct other men and women.

1st John 2:18-29 tells us:

> *"Little children, it is the last hour; and as you have heard that the Antichrist is coming, even now many antichrists have come, by which we know that it is the last hour. They went out from us, but they were not of us; for if they had been of us, they would have continued with us; but they went out that they might be made manifest, that*

none of them were of us.

But you have an anointing from the Holy One, and you know all things. I have not written to you because you do not know the truth, but because you know it, and that no lie is of the truth.

Who is a liar but he who denies that Jesus is the Christ? He is antichrist who denies the Father and the Son. Whoever denies the Son does not have the Father either; he who acknowledges the Son has the Father also.

Therefore let that abide in you which you heard from the beginning. If what you heard from the beginning abides in you, you also will abide in the Son and in the Father. And this is the promise that He has promised us—eternal life.

These things I have written to you concerning those who try to deceive you. But the anointing which you have received from Him abides in you, and you do not need that anyone teach you; but as the same anointing teaches you concerning all things, and is true, and is not a lie, and just as it has taught you, you will abide in Him.

And now, little children, abide in Him, that when He appears, we may have confidence and not be ashamed before Him at His coming. If you know that He is righteous, you know that everyone who practices righteousness is born of Him."

Christ is our ultimate authority. There are to be no "Lone Rangers" in the Body of Christ. Many people who have been using drugs and alcohol tend to be isolationists, especially once they stop taking their synthetic courage. All of us need to stretch ourselves to be part of the Body of Christ.

I am often asked the question, "Does going to church make you a Christian?" My answer to that is, "Not any more than going to the Elk's Club makes you an elk or going to McDonald's makes you a hamburger. But, we are commanded to be in fellowship." The writer of Hebrews shares this in Hebrews 10:22-26:

> *"Let us draw near with a true heart in full assurance of faith, having our hearts sprinkled from an evil conscience and our bodies washed with pure water. Let us hold fast the confession of our hope without wavering, for He who promised is faithful. And let us consider one another in order to stir up love and good works, not forsaking the assembling of ourselves together, as is the manner of some, but exhorting one another, and so much the more as you see the Day approaching. For if we sin willfully after we have received the knowledge of the truth, there no longer remains a sacrifice for sins."*

This passage is actually telling us the closer we get to Christ's return, the more we need each other's support. To grow and mature in our Christian walk, we need a cross-section of support. One person illustrated this by describing the cross in a certain way. As you look at a cross, the top limb of the vertical beam represents having someone over you. Allowing spiritual authority to be over us from our mentors and spiritual parents is a critical part of growing spiritually. The horizontal crossbeam extended out to the left and right, represents having spiritual peers we are growing up in Christ with. These people are the ones that are on the same spiritual plane with us. Lastly, we have the bottom vertical limb of the cross that represents someone we are mentoring in the faith. This person is someone younger in the faith that we are imparting with what has been taught to us by our mentors, and what we have learned from our own experiences.

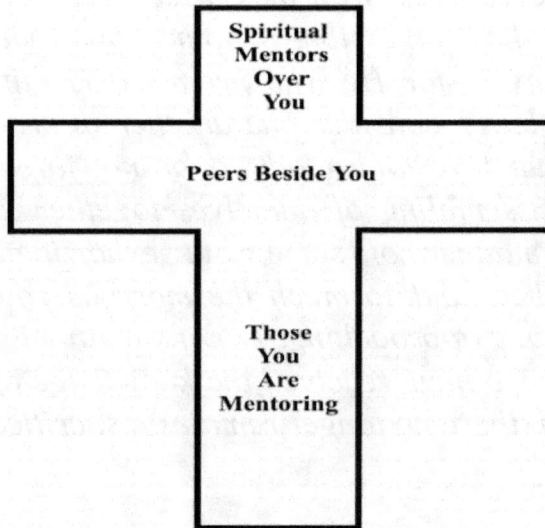

Spiritual
Mentors
Over
You

Peers Beside You

Those
You
Are
Mentoring

God has set the church spiritual leadership in place to help us grow in our Christian walk. These leaders operate in the spiritual offices of Apostle, Prophet, Evangelist, Pastor, and Teacher. We read about this in Ephesians 4:11-16:

> *"And He Himself gave some to be apostles, some prophets, some evangelists, and some pastors and teachers, for the equipping of the saints for the work of ministry, for the edifying of the body of Christ, till we all come to the unity of the faith and of the knowledge of the Son of God, to a perfect man, to the measure of the stature of the fullness of Christ; that we should no longer be children, tossed to and fro and carried about with every wind of doctrine, by the trickery of men, in the cunning craftiness of deceitful plotting, but, speaking the truth in love, may grow up in all things into Him who is the head—Christ—from whom the whole body, joined and knit together by what every joint supplies, according to the effective working by which every part does its share, causes growth of the body for the edifying of itself in love."*

It is our responsibility to find and develop relationships with the most Godly men and women with whom we can be associated. This is of utmost importance because we will tend only to be as holy as the people we associate with.

God expects us to develop trusting relationships with the spiritual mentors He has brought into our lives. We all need people to be accountable to. If we have never really been transparent with anyone this can be hard to do at first, especially if we have been deeply hurt by those who have misused the authority they had over our lives. However, when the Lord brings Godly people into our lives, we need to take the advantage of the opportunity and give them access to our heart. Godly people only have our best interests in mind. They realize that they too, are accountable to God.

Hebrews 13:17 tells us:

"Obey them that have the rule over you, and submit yourselves: for they watch for your souls, as they that must give account, that they may do it with joy, and not with grief: for that is unprofitable for you." (ASV)

And James 3:1:

"My brethren, be not many masters, knowing that we shall receive the greater condemnation."

We are exhorted by God to be committed and submitted to a local body of believers. We need to become part of a living organism—the Church. The Apostle Paul writes in 1st Corinthians 12:13-17, 20-21:

> *"For by one Spirit we were all baptized into one body—whether Jews or Greeks, whether slaves or free—and have all been made to drink into one Spirit. For in fact the body is not one member but many.*
>
> *If the foot should say, "Because I am not a hand, I am not of the body," is it therefore not of the body? And if the ear should say, "Because I am not an eye, I am not of the body," is it therefore not of the body? If the whole body were an eye, where would be the hearing? If the whole were hearing, where would be the smelling?*
>
> *But now indeed there are many members, yet one body. And the eye cannot say to the hand, "I have no need of you"; nor again the head to the feet, "I have no need of you."*

It's not easy to be submitted and committed to those around us. Our pride and self-centeredness always wants to get in the way. This is especially true of people who have struggled with compulsory behaviors. However, it is paramount that we understand the necessity of learning commitment and submission to our spiritual mentors. No doubt, rebellion to authority is one of the key issues that needs to be addressed in our lives. This is especially true of someone who has been incarcerated a number of times.

Some people think if someone has done time well, they have learned their lesson, but this is not necessarily true. Most seasoned offenders learn how to work their programs inside an institution in order to get released, but still have rebellion raging inside them. It's like the story of the young child who was told by his mother he needed to sit in the corner for his misbehavior. The child went to the corner and sat on his chair as his mother requested. Once seated, he looked at his mother and said, "I may be sitting down on the outside, but I'm standing up on the inside!" Can you relate to this?

Previously, we looked at the importance of restoring our family relationships. Most people who struggle with addiction and incarceration issues have not ever learned how to function in a family environment. This is why learning how to relate well with our church family is so important. We will never be able to function well in the "world's society" if we cannot learn how to function in our "church family."

Granted, some family members are easier to love than others. Remember, you can choose your friends, but you're "stuck" with your relatives, which include your family in Christ. God has designed it this way so that we will stay sharpened tools for the Lord to use. Proverbs 27:17 tells us:

"As iron sharpens iron, So a man

sharpens the countenance of his friend."

God desires that we develop deep relationships: Proverbs 27:6 tells us:

> *"Faithful are the wounds of a friend; but the kisses of an enemy are deceitful."*

God builds character in us mainly through relationships. Sometimes relationships bring pain. Life is full of challenges whether we are believers or unbelievers. We can suffer in the world and receive the world's reward, or we can suffer in the Church and receive the Lord's reward. That is what the writer of Hebrews was saying in Hebrews 11:24-25 where he penned:

> *"By faith Moses, when he was come to years, refused to be called the son of Pharaoh's daughter; Choosing rather to suffer affliction with the people of God, than to enjoy the pleasures of sin for a season;"*

No one can see the whole picture. We especially can't see it when we are in it. We need our brothers and sisters in Christ to help us keep a clear perspective of what's going on around us.

Sometimes it takes awhile to find the right church and the best spiritual mentors. But keep asking, seeking, and knocking on doors until you do. God encourages us to do so. He will lead us in the right direction until what we really need happens. The Lord will often make us work at something, so we can appreciate its value. A church that God leads you to will not be bondage to you but will bring you life and peace.

The Lord's "True Church" does not manipulate the children of God. The church is never encouraged to control you in any way but is encouraged to nourish, protect, and grow you into the image of Christ. If you have had a bad experience with an organization claiming to be the church, be thick skinned and press on. The right church for you may be on the next corner.

A good pastor and church will heed to what the Apostle Peter wrote in 1st Peter 5:1-7:

> *"The elders who are among you I exhort, I who am a fellow elder and a witness of the sufferings of Christ, and also a partaker of the glory that will be revealed: Shepherd the flock of God which is among you, serving as overseers, not by compulsion but willingly, not for dishonest gain but eagerly; nor as being lords over those entrusted to you, but being examples to the flock; and when the Chief Shepherd appears, you will receive the crown of glory that does not fade away.*
>
> *Likewise you younger people, submit yourselves to your elders. Yes, all of you be submissive to one another, and be clothed*

with humility, for

'God resists the proud, But gives grace to the humble.'

Therefore humble yourselves under the mighty hand of God, that He may exalt you in due time, casting all your care upon Him, for He cares for you."

Homework

Return this homework assignment to the instructor of this class before the next lesson. If possible, also make a copy of this page for your own reference.

1. Has the Lord spoken anything to you from this lesson? If so, what?

_____

_____

_____

_____

2. What practical applications from this lesson or chapter apply to you?

_____

_____

_____

_____

Chapter Five
Our Occupations—Bread Winning

From the beginning of creation, God intended man to have a job. We read in Genesis 2:15-17:

> *"Then the LORD God took the man and put him in the garden of Eden to tend and keep it. And the LORD God commanded the man, saying, "Of every tree of the garden you may freely eat; but of the tree of the knowledge of good and evil you shall not eat, for in the day that you eat of it you shall surely die."*

Right from the get-go, man was put in charge of maintaining the Garden of Eden and governing the world around him. In Genesis we are told the creation story, and that all that God created was good. God created Adam to till the soil in peace and harmony with Him. This tending of the Garden was the main responsibility that God had given Adam. The Bible would later call this type of responsibility–stewardship. In 1st Corinthians 4:1, and other passages in the Bible, we are told that it is important that we take seriously the stewardship God has given to us. Sometimes the Bible addresses the importance of stewardship in regard to practical goods, and sometimes it is referred to in the context of spiritual responsibilities.

God let Adam know up front that there would certainly be negative consequences if he ignored God's commandments. I think you know the story of what happened next. It was not long before Adam and Eve, encouraged by the devil, disobeyed God's command-ments and ate from the tree of knowledge of good and evil. The results of this disobedience brought many spiritual and physical consequences. Genesis 3:17-19 tells us specifically about these consequences:

> *"Then to Adam He said, "Because you have heeded the voice of your wife, and have eaten from the tree of which I commanded you, saying, 'You shall not eat of it': "Cursed is the ground for your sake; In toil you shall eat of it. All the days of your life. Both thorns and thistles it shall bring forth for you, And you shall eat the herb of the field. In the sweat of your face you shall eat bread Till you return to the ground, For out of it you were taken; For dust you are, And to dust you shall return."*

One of the consequences for Adam and Eve was increased labor in man tilling the soil and increased labor in women in bearing children. We are often mystified, sometimes angered, at why God created in the way that He did. Why did He even leave the ability for us to sin? Why the harsh consequences?

I believe God's intention in this was to give men and

women a lifelong reminder of the value of what they lost, and an appreciation for what they could re-establish. God always provides a way for redemption.

I heard an interview with Oprah Winfrey and Sylvester Stallone. Something that Stallone said stuck with me that illustrated this point. Oprah was reminding Stallone of the tremendous uphill climb he had in his career. All his life, Stallone had been ridiculed about his poor speaking qualities and looks, by most of the movie industry. Yet he was not deterred and pursued his dream of acting and directing. Twenty-five years later, after much hard work and persistence, Stallone was at the height of stardom. He was making hundreds of millions of dollars. Women were swooning over him. After describing this struggle, Oprah's question to Stallone was something like, "Now that you have experienced the rags-to-riches scenario, what is your biggest fear?" Without hesitation, Stallone said his biggest fear was that his son would never realize what it took to get to the place where his family is now. Get it?

In other words, Adam and Eve never knew how good they had it. Appreciation probably was not in their vocabulary. Up to the fall in the Garden, they never knew any true hardship. At the end of their days however, they certainly could look back at the loss. But also, they could look forward in appreciation for what the Lord had taught them through it. Working at something helps us appreciate what we have earned. The harder the task, the more we appreciate our accomplishments.

Now, we are not to judge our work standards according to the world, especially the standards of our

Western (American) civilization. Each culture in the world has developed its own work standards. Working 9-to-5 Monday through Friday is not Godly or ungodly. Working the swing or graveyard shift is not Godly or ungodly (although some shifts may keep you from having a healthy Christian social life). Working nine months out of the year and taking three months off is not Godly or ungodly. What God does expect of us, is to be financially responsible. Let me say this again with emphasis, *"Financial Responsibility"* is more important than when you punch a time clock.

I need to let you know something. Nowhere in the Bible have I read about God giving anyone the spiritual gift of receiving. However, some people live their lives as though they have been given this gift. Friends, God wants us to be contributors, not takers.

The Apostle Paul makes this clear in 2nd Thessalonians 3:6-15:

> *"But we command you, brethren, in the name of our Lord Jesus Christ, that you withdraw from every brother who walks disorderly and not according to the tradition which he received from us. For you yourselves know how you ought to follow us, for we were not disorderly among you; nor did we eat anyone's bread free of charge, but worked with labor and toil night and day, that we might not be a burden to any of you, not because we do not have authority, but to make ourselves an example of how*

you should follow us.

For even when we were with you, we commanded you this: If anyone will not work, neither shall he eat. For we hear that there are some who walk among you in a disorderly manner, not working at all, but are busybodies. Now those who are such we command and exhort through our Lord Jesus Christ that they work in quietness and eat their own bread.

But as for you, brethren, do not grow weary in doing good. And if anyone does not obey our word in this epistle, note that person and do not keep company with him, that he may be ashamed. Yet do not count him as an enemy, but admonish him as a brother."

Does this mean that God expects you to be working a full-time job the day you start your rehabilitation journey? My answer is yes and no. For some, full-time employment right away is a necessary step in their recovery process. However, for those who have spent significant time unemployed, abusing drugs and alcohol or incarcerated, the answer for most is no. God often gives those in the process of restoration a special time of grace to work on the immediate issues that will be foundational to rehabilitation. This special time could be days, weeks, or months. Whatever the situation or wherever a person may be residing, he must become a contributor as soon as possible. If a person does not learn how to do this in their present circumstance, they won't do it elsewhere later.

Some people coming out of prison or long-term addiction have virtually no work skills, and they know it. This of course can cause anxiety and fear. Sometimes the fear of failure or having to become responsible is so overwhelming it will drive this type of person right back into incarceration or chemical dependency. We must combat fear with faith. As newborn babes in faith, we need to learn to trust in God's awesome love for us. No matter where we are in our maturity in the natural or spiritual, we can trust in God. The bottom line is if we give our heart, soul, mind, and spirit to God, He is able to take care of us. Matthew 6:33 tells us if we are seeking God first in our lives, He will provide for us. Jesus said He came to give us abundant life in John 10:10. The Bible also tells us that we were created to enjoy the fruit of our labor in Psalm 128:1-2.

When it comes to choosing vocations and ministries, we often ask the question, "What is God's will for me?" I think this is a good question. We should always ask God's advice on all things. However, I think more often than not, God is also asking us, "What is your heart's desire?"

The Bible illustrates that there have been some men and women called by God to a specific vocation or ministry. Most of us will not hear from God that specifically. He expects us to learn His scriptures and then make Godly decisions accordingly. If our will is to do God's will, according to His instructions in the Bible, we can choose a profession, spouse, or ministry that is glorifying to God, and expect Him to stand with us. Proverbs 16:9 tells us that God is always leading us. If we are not making the right decisions in any of those areas, God will always intervene through His Word, His Body, or His Spirit by bringing us better direction. That is, of course, only if we are open to hear His correction.

Psalm 37:4 tells us:

"Delight yourself in the Lord, feed on His faithfulness and He shall give you the desires of your heart."

There has been a debate among Christians throughout time on how these desires get into our hearts. Are they imparted by God only; or are they part of our own creating and choosing? I think they are a mix of both. If they are Godly desires that can be supported in the Bible, we need not be too concerned on how they get there. Our responsibility is to pursue Godly desires, and we will see them become a reality. The bottom line is, choose something you like doing, and ask God to help you get there.

Jesus said:

"Take my yoke upon you, and learn of me; for I am meek and lowly in heart, and ye shall find rest unto your souls. For my yoke is easy, and my burden is light." (Matthew 11:29-30)

God will help find the best job for YOU. As you

pursue your dream vocation, be practical. We are not all supposed to be singing on Broadway, especially if you can't carry a tune! Hard work (diligence) is still the key to prosperity. Few ever will win the lottery!

1st Timothy 6:9 says:

> *"People who want to get rich fall into temptation and a trap and into many foolish and harmful desires that plunge men into ruin and destruction."*

Remember to be flexible. Your idea of the perfect job and God's idea might be a little different.

The Apostle Paul was one of the main people in the Bible who God called to be an example of a Christian man. His heart's desire was to be a minister. He especially wanted to minister to his countrymen, the Jews. But God had a different plan for Paul and called him to be the Apostle to the Gentiles (Romans 11:13). Paul wanted to be in the ministry once he received Christ, but he spent 10 to 14 years as a tent-maker, waiting for the Lord's calling. Paul was a traveler, but God had him spend a lot of time in jail. Unknown to Paul at the time, while incarcerated, he would be used to accomplish much more ministry than if he was traveling around the country.

The Lord will help you get into the area of work and ministry for which you are best suited. Be patient and diligent at what He has set before you right now. He may be doing something through you that you are not even aware of yet.

Homework

Return this homework to the instructor of this class before the next lesson. If possible, also make a copy of this page for your own reference.

1. Write down three occupations you would like to have.

_____

_____

_____

_____

2. If you are not in one of these now, write down why not and three steps you could take to get closer to obtaining the position you want to have.

_____

_____

_____

_____

_____

_____

_____

3. Ask God daily to help you complete your three steps.

__Notes__

Chapter Six
Our Financial Lives–What We Do With Our Money

In the previous chapter, we discussed the importance of working and becoming a contributor and not a taker. We saw in the Bible how the Lord wanted us to secure a vocation or a job. This is an important first step in developing financial responsibility, but it is only one step in the path we must walk down.

A life of chemical abuse or crime always leaves a wake of financial disaster. For those who have grown up in dysfunctional homes, where there has not been a model of financial responsibility, this will be one of the disciplines that will take time and effort to learn. Once learned, it will lead to financial success and freedom, which will be well worth the effort.

I believe the bottom line to being financially responsible is achieved by applying these two rules:

1. Pay your bills on time.
2. Do not spend more money than you make.

The Lord makes this very clear in the book of Romans:

"Therefore, it is necessary to submit to the authorities, not only because of possible punishment but also because of conscience.

This is also why you pay taxes, for the authorities are God's servants, who give their full time to governing. Give everyone what you owe him: If you owe taxes, pay taxes; if revenue, then revenue; if respect, then respect; if honor, then honor. <u>Let no debt remain outstanding</u>, except the continuing debt to love one another, for he who loves his fellowman has fulfilled the law."(Romans 13:5-8 NIV)

There has been much discussion on whether Christians should or should not borrow money. Today with the price of cars and houses being so high, it seems almost unavoidable. Some churches teach (though very few) that Christians should always pay cash for everything; that buying anything with credit is not in God's will. I don't hold to such a stringent interpretation of this scripture.

I believe credit can be used as a tool for God's kingdom. Credit can be useful when purchasing items that appreciate in value such as property or a home. But, if used incorrectly, this tool can cause more harm than good. Should you decided to buy on credit, keep the rules, "Pay your bills on time," and "Do not spend more money than you make," and you will always have a guard to keep you from overextending yourself. Personally, I use a credit card; however, I always pay it off each month. If I find that I cannot do this, I know that I am overextending God's provision for me. I believe when we overextend, we are most likely entering into sin and financial irresponsibility.

God expects us to maintain a good witness in handling our finances. The Lord talked about finances more than any other subject in the Bible, except for the doctrine of eternal retribution (hell). He emphasized again and again that we should be a good steward of all God has given us. A steward is a person who is in charge of another's property. Jesus used many parables to illustrate the importance of good stewardship. In fact, if we study the connection between financial irresponsibility and losing out on eternal life, it is very sobering. This correlation is not just reserved for those who have been ruined financially because of poor financial choices, but it also relates to those who have the world's riches and do not use them for the kingdom's sake.

In the parable of the talents in Matthew 25:14-30, and the parable of pounds or minas in Luke 19:11-27, Jesus shares about the rewards and punishments that are directly related to how we were or were not good stewards of what He has given us. Though the stories are somewhat similar, there are some significant differences in these parables too. In the parable of the talents, God gives different measures to the stewards. But in the parable of the pounds, He gives the same measure to all. I believe this is significant because in Matthew it indicates we are not to be concerned about how many talents or skills we have, but to be diligent with what we have been given.

Don't look at what God gives someone else; just be faithful to grow what He has given you. In Luke's story, everyone gets the same amount. This refers to the fact that we all get the same amount of time, or twenty-four hours a day to invest in God's kingdom. The bottom line in both stories is, God expects us to use what He gives us responsibly.

So, what are some of the ways we should invest in the kingdom of God? We will cover this next.

First of all, we need to talk about tithing. Tithing is a term used for describing giving 10% of your financial increase back to God. The Bible tells us God gives us all things and gives us the ability to earn what we have. He then asks us to give 10% back to Him. This is to be given to the priests and pastors who are called to full-time ministry. The tithe frees up priests and pastors to work full-time in the temple or church. The New Testament says that ministers who labor in prayer and instructing the congregation about the Word of God should be paid twice as much as the normal salary. (1st Timothy 5:17-18)

The revelation of tithing was given prophetically prior to the Mosaic Law or before the time of Moses. We read in Genesis that Abraham tithed:

> *"After Abram returned from defeating Kedorlaomer and the kings allied with him, the king of Sodom came out to meet him in the Valley of Shaveh (that is, the King's Valley). Then Melchizedek king of Salem brought out bread and wine. He was priest of God Most High, and he blessed Abram, saying, "Blessed be Abram by God Most*

High, Creator of heaven and earth. And blessed be God Most High, who delivered your enemies into your hand. "Then Abram gave him a tenth of everything." (Genesis 14:17-20 NIV)

We also find in the Bible that Jacob had a revelation of tithing from his increase:

"Early the next morning Jacob took the stone he had placed under his head and set it up as a pillar and poured oil on top of it. He called that place Bethel, though the city used to be called Luz. Then Jacob made a vow, saying, "If God will be with me and will watch over me on this journey I am taking and will give me food to eat and clothes to wear so that I return safely to my father's house, then the LORD will be my God and this stone that I have set up as a pillar will be God's house, and of all that you give me I will give you a tenth." (Genesis 28:18-22 NIV)

Clearer revelation of the tithe came with the Mosaic Law. This was the law given to Moses to govern the Jews (the children of Israel). When the children of Israel went into Canaan, the Promised Land, God gave inheritances of the land to all the tribes of Israel except the tribe of Levi. God ordained all the Levites to the work of ministry full-time. The Levites would work hand-in-hand with the priests in the temple, with daily chores and offering of sacrifices. We read in Leviticus that tithes from all increases belong to God and should be given right away. If anyone dedicated something to the Lord and then wanted to substitute the item for something else, he would have to give the full worth in material goods or money to the temple plus 20% of the total worth. We see this in Leviticus where Moses wrote,

> *"<u>A tithe of everything from the land, whether grain from the soil or fruit from the trees, belongs to the LORD; it is holy to the LORD</u>. If a man redeems any of his tithe, he must add a fifth of the value to it. The entire tithe of the herd and flock--every tenth animal that passes under the shepherd's rod--will be holy to the LORD. He must not pick out the good from the bad or make any substitution. If he does make a substitution, both the animal and its substitute become holy and cannot be redeemed." (Leviticus 27:30-33 NIV)*

Although tithing in the Old Testament was important, it was never the way to salvation. It would not save your soul, but tithing can save you some money. What's that, you say? How can giving my money away save me money? Take a look at what God tells us in Malachi:

> *"Will a man rob God? Yet you rob me.*

"But you ask, 'How do we rob you?' "In tithes and offerings. You are under a curse-- the whole nation of you--because you are robbing me. Bring the whole tithe into the storehouse, that there may be food in my house. Test me in this," says the LORD Almighty, "and see if I will not throw open the floodgates of heaven and pour out so much blessing that you will not have room enough for it. <u>I will prevent pests from devouring your crops, and the vines in your fields will not cast their fruit," says the LORD Almighty.</u> "Then all the nations will call you blessed, for yours will be a delightful land," says the LORD Almighty." (Malachi 3:8-12 NIV)

Get it? If they wanted God to protect their money, they needed to do what He said. Otherwise God told them they were spending their money according to the financial plan of the Devil. He warned them that if they would not give to God's kingdom, eventually they would lose all that they had to the kingdom of the enemy.

I think we can see clearly that the tithe was established in the Old Testament as the provision for the ministers to take care of congregations of the Lord. We also can see that God promised a blessing to all those who would honor the tithe. But is it a New Testament requirement? Are we not free from the Old Testament Laws?

As mentioned before, the tithe was to go to the

priests and Levites for their inheritance. No one was exempt from tithing. Even the Levites and Priests were to tithe to the High Priest as we can see in the 18th Chapter of the book of Numbers:

"I give to the Levites all the tithes in Israel as their inheritance in return for the work they do while serving at the Tent of Meeting. From now on the Israelites must not go near the Tent of Meeting, or they will bear the consequences of their sin and will die. It is the Levites who are to do the work at the Tent of Meeting and bear the responsibility for offenses against it. This is a lasting ordinance for the generations to come. They will receive no inheritance among the Israelites. Instead, I give to the Levites as their inheritance the tithes that the Israelites present as an offering to the LORD. That is why I said concerning them: 'They will have no inheritance among the Israelites.'" The LORD said to Moses, "Speak to the Levites and say to them: 'When you receive from the Israelites the tithe I give you as your inheritance, you must present a tenth of that tithe as the Lord's offering. Your offering will be reckoned to you as grain from the threshing floor or juice from the winepress. In this way you also will present an offering to the LORD from all the tithes you receive from

the Israelites. From these tithes you must give the Lord's portion to Aaron the priest." (Numbers 18:21-28 NIV)

The High Priest was a kind of Christ that reflected the true Christ who was to come. In other words, the tithing that was commanded in the Old Testament was an example of how we should bless Christ with our finances in the New Testament. This also is supported in the story we looked at earlier about Abraham giving tithes to Melchizedek, King of Salem. The book of Hebrews tells us that Melchizedek also reflected and modeled Christ. The prophetic picture we have been given is pretty clear. Nowhere in the New Testament do we see that the tithe was to be discontinued.

There is a story I like to tell to further illustrate this. There was a couple celebrating their 50th wedding anniversary. As they sat together at a nice restaurant for dinner, the woman looked lovingly into her husband's eyes and said, "Honey, thank you for sharing your life with me in marriage for fifty years. I have been very happy, but I have one concern I would like to share with you. My concern is this, you never tell me you love me any more." The man responded, "Darling, when we got married I told you I loved you, and if I ever change my mind, I'll let you know."

Get it? If the Lord had a change in plans for providing for those He has called to the ministry, I believe He would have let us know clearly.

When Jesus came on the scene, He shared many examples with his disciples on how the Mosaic Law was no longer applicable, but He never indicated this was true of the tithe. Nowhere in the New Testament do we find the word "tithe" but nowhere do we find a specific mention of the tithe being done away with. Instead it implies in the Gospel of Matthew that Jesus specifically supported the tithe while addressing the Pharisees:

> *"Woe to you, teachers of the law and Pharisees, you hypocrites! You give a tenth of your spices--mint, dill and cummin. But you have neglected the more important matters of the law--justice, mercy and faithfulness. <u>You should have practiced the latter, without neglecting the former.</u>" (Matthew 23:23 NIV)*

Also, I believe the Apostle Paul taught about the importance of tithing in the New Testament. In his letters to the Corinthian Church, Paul teaches the principle of the tithe supporting those called to full-time ministry was still commanded:

> *"Who serves as a soldier at his own expense? Who plants a vineyard and does not eat of its grapes? Who tends a flock and does not drink of the milk? Do I say this merely from a human point of view? Doesn't the Law say the same thing? For it is written in the Law of Moses: "Do not muzzle an ox while it is treading out the grain." Is it about oxen that God is concerned? Surely he says*

this for us, doesn't he? Yes, this was written for us, because when the plowman plows and the thresher threshes, they ought to do so in the hope of sharing in the harvest. If we have sown spiritual seed among you, is it too much if we reap a material harvest from you? If others have this right of support from you, shouldn't we have it all the more? But we did not use this right. On the contrary, we put up with anything rather than hinder the gospel of Christ. <u>Don't you know that those who work in the temple get their food from the temple, and those who serve at the altar share in what is offered on the altar? In the same way, the Lord has commanded that those who preach the gospel should receive their living from the gospel.</u>" (1st Corinthians 9:1-14 NIV)

Paul did not use the word tithe here. He also did not want to personally receive support at this time in his ministry, but he clearly taught that God wanted the church to support His full-time ministers. Paul again teaches in 1st Timothy the importance of the tithe for providing for the needs of elders who are preaching and teaching:

"<u>The elders who direct the affairs of the church well are worthy of double honor, especially those whose work is preaching and teaching.</u> For the Scripture says, "Do

not muzzle the ox while it is treading out the grain," and "The worker deserves his wages." (1st Timothy 5:17-18 NIV)

Some Bible teachers say that the above passages are just encouragement in giving with no specific amount specified. They often balance their belief with some scriptures Paul wrote in 2nd Corinthians that we will look at momentarily. These scriptures however, are not addressing the tithe but instruct us how to give free will offerings.

The tithe has always been designated for those who are called to the ministry by God. But as just mentioned, we are also to give free will offerings for the poor and needy. These gifts are separate from the tithe. Giving of free will offerings was demonstrated in the Old Testament as well as the New Testament.

In the New Testament, the Apostle Paul teaches about free will offerings in 2nd Corinthians Chapter Eight.

"For if the willingness is there, the gift is acceptable according to what one has, not according to what he does not have. Our desire is not that others might be relieved while you are hard pressed, but that there might be equality. At the present time your plenty will supply what they need, so that in turn their plenty will supply what you need. Then there will be equality, as it is written: "He who gathered much did not have too much, and he who gathered little did not

have too little." (2nd Corinthians 8:12-15 NIV)

"So I thought it necessary to urge the brothers to visit you in advance and finish the arrangements for the generous gift you had promised. Then it will be ready as a generous gift, not as one grudgingly given. Remember this: Whoever sows sparingly will also reap sparingly, and whoever sows generously will also reap generously. Each man should give what he has decided in his heart to give, not reluctantly or under compulsion, for God loves a cheerful giver. And God is able to make all grace abound to you, so that in all things at all times, having all that you need, you will abound in every good work. As it is written: "He has scattered abroad his gifts to the poor; his righteousness endures forever." (2nd Corinthians 9:5-9 NIV)

In conclusion of this chapter, I want to say no matter what you believe about tithing, one thing is for sure, God wants us to be givers. He also wants us to keep a loose hold on our material possessions. Jesus taught us this clearly in the Gospel of Matthew where we read,

"Do not store up for yourselves treasures on earth, where moth and rust destroy, and where thieves break in and steal. But store up for yourselves

treasures in heaven, where moth and rust do not destroy, and where thieves do not break in and steal. <u>For where your treasure is, there your heart will be also.</u>"
(Matthew 6:19-21 NIV)

So where is your treasure? Does it belong to God or to you? If God has your money, He also has your heart!

My encouragement to you is to start giving now, even if it is not much. If you can't discipline yourself to give of what you have now, you probably won't do it later when you think you'll have enough to give.

Lastly, I want to leave you with three principles that God has instituted concerning giving. They have been called the "Reaping Principles" by some. They can be found in Galatians 6:7-10, and 2nd Corinthians 9:6.

1. We will reap what we sow.
2. We will reap more than what we sow.
3. We are always sowing something.

So my last question to you is, what are you sowing?

Homework

1. Tithe for three months.

2. Keep a diary of what happened with your finances during those three months. You may make some notes here also.

_____

_____

_____

_____

_____

_____

_____

_____

_____

3. Share your experiences monthly with the group or your spiritual mentor.

<u>Notes</u>

Chapter Seven
Our Social Lives

Many of us bring our bad habits and hang-ups into the kingdom of God. This chapter focuses on some of these, particularly in the context of what it means to fit into society. The society we are talking about is twofold: the Church or spiritual kingdom of God, and secular society, the world that we live in.

It is highly important that we keep the focus of this study on ourselves and not others. Don't ask the Lord to bring revelation to someone else. Ask the Lord to bring revelation to you. We need to fix ourselves before we approach others. Jesus said this clearly when He taught the Sermon on the Mount:

"Do not judge, or you too will be judged. For in the same way you judge others, you will be judged, and with the measure you use, it will be measured to you. "Why do you look at the speck of sawdust in your brother's eye and pay no attention to the plank in your own eye? How can you say to your brother, 'Let me take the speck out of your eye,' when all the time there is a plank in your own eye? You hypocrite, first take the plank out of your own eye, and then you will see clearly to remove the speck from your brother's eye."(Matthew 7:1-5 NIV)

Do you want the Lord to judge you the way you judge others? Do you really meet all of the requirements you hold of others perfectly? Remember that when you point the finger at someone, there are three pointing back at you. If we're honest, we will admit we all want and need grace! What is grace? One definition is, **G**ods **R**iches **A**t **C**hrist's **E**xpense. So again, please keep the focus of this study on what the Lord wants to change in you.

We all have things we have to work through. Most likely, before you were a Christian, you were self-centered. You probably conducted yourself in anti-social or non-conformist ways to get attention. Or you may have acted in anti-social ways to keep people away from you. Now that you are a new creature in Christ, (2nd Corinthians 5:17) God wants you to become part of the family of God. He also wants you to connect with those in the secular society around you, without engaging in its sinful activities.

Many of us wonder why people are looking at us strangely or why we sense we are not accepted by a particular segment of society. Have you really taken an honest look at your self? Perhaps your habits or hang-ups are alienating you. Perhaps people have even persecuted you and you wonder why.

I was mentoring one brother who was out of prison. He had several face piercings and tattoos. Yet he shared with me that he felt like people did not accept him. It bothered him that people were always staring at him. Well duh! I told him if he didn't want people to stare at him, to take out his earrings and wear long sleeve shirts when at work.

God hasn't called us to be weird! If we are to be persecuted it's supposed to be because of righteousness' sake and not because we dress or act obnoxiously. Jesus in the Sermon on the Mount said:

"Blessed are those who are persecuted because of righteousness, for theirs is the kingdom of heaven. "Blessed are you when people insult you, persecute you and falsely say all kinds of evil against you because of me. Rejoice and be glad, because great is your reward in heaven, for in the same way they persecuted the prophets who were before you." (Matthew 5:10-12 NIV)

Christians are supposed to blend into society. Jesus did. What made Jesus stand out in a room was He walked in truth, in love, and in power. Besides that, you couldn't pick him out in a crowd. Judas had to identify Christ in the midst of His disciples with a kiss. Otherwise the Romans would not have known whom to arrest. We read about this in the gospel of Luke:

"Why are you sleeping?" he asked them. "Get up and pray so that you will not fall into temptation." While he was still speaking a crowd came up, and the man who was called Judas, one of the Twelve, was leading them. He approached Jesus to kiss him, but Jesus asked him, "Judas, are

you betraying the Son of Man with a kiss?"
(Luke 22:46-48 NIV)

Paul the Apostle blended into society like Jesus.
Read what he wrote about himself in 1st Corinthians:

"Though I am free and belong to no
man, I make myself a slave to everyone, to
win as many as possible. To the Jews I
became like a Jew, to win the Jews. To those
under the law I became like one under the
law (though I myself am not under the law),
so as to win those under the law. To those
not having the law I became like one not
having the law (though I am not free from
God's law but am under Christ's law), so as
to win those not having the law. To the weak
I became weak, to win the weak. I have
become all things to all men so that by all
possible means I might save some. I do all
this for the sake of the gospel, that I may
share in its blessings." (1st Corinthians 9:19-
23 NIV)

Paul knew the importance of blending in with a
culture. He wanted to connect with the people for the
Gospel's sake in any society he was in, as long as he
could do it without compromising the scriptures.

I am not saying that we are all to look and act the
same. Some people call that being just a cookie-cutter
Christian. God does not take away our personalities. He

does however take away anything in us that distracts us or others from His kingdom.

Sometimes the Lord will call us to reach out to a different culture as He did with James Hudson Taylor. James was an Englishman who took on the dress and look of a Chinaman when he ministered in China. This was very offensive to his fellow English missionaries in China. They felt it was degrading to lower one's self to the heathen dress of the Chinese. James had to offend his missionary brethren because he felt compelled by God to take on Chinese dress to evangelize in China.

I personally came out of an outlaw motorcycle club culture. For the first few years of my Christian walk, I still rode and looked the part of an outlaw biker. However, now I was riding and witnessing for Jesus. Eventually, God had me lay down the ministry in that fashion. But He has others who are called to this type of evangelism as their regular ministry. As long as we are doing what we do for the glory of Christ (not to bring attention to ourselves) I give a big AMEN! There will be situations where we may offend our own culture or someone else's culture. However, I believe the Bible teaches that we should only do this when the Lord is clearly leading us to go against society's norm.

Another area I would like to touch is why it is important to obey the civil law. I will share more on this subject in our last lesson. The Bible teaches us to blend into society. Blending into society means keeping society's rules. The Apostle Peter wrote:

"Dear friends, I urge you, as aliens and

strangers in the world, to abstain from sinful desires, which war against your soul. Live such good lives among the pagans that, though they accuse you of doing wrong, they may see your good deeds and glorify God on the day he visits us. Submit yourselves for the Lord's sake to every authority instituted among men: whether to the king, as the supreme authority, or to governors, who are sent by him to punish those who do wrong and to commend those who do right. For it is God's will that by doing good you should silence the ignorant talk of foolish men. Live as free men, but do not use your freedom as a cover-up for evil; live as servants of God. Show proper respect to everyone: Love the brotherhood of believers, fear God, honor the king." (1ˢᵗ Peter 2:11-17 NIV)

Paul also wrote:

"Everything is permissible--but not everything is beneficial. Everything is permissible—but not everything is constructive." (1ˢᵗ Corinthians 10:23 NIV)

Christ has not called us to rebel against society or the church. Instead of "bucking the system," we are to do our best to be constructive and complement the world around us without compromising our walk in Christ. For some of us, it is very difficult to feel like we fit into society, but Christ has not called us to be hermits. We are to be in the world but not of the world. While we are here, Jesus promises to take care of us (John 17:15-17). God tells us that we can even learn to feel safe around our enemies. Proverbs 16:7 promises us, *"When the ways of people please the LORD, He makes even their enemies live at peace with them."*

Almost everyone I know wants to have more peace in his or her life. Often we don't experience peace or cut ourselves short of the peace we could have because we are being obnoxious in some way. We may not even be aware of the things we are neglecting in our lives, so that's why it is important that we give close friends who love us, permission to give us constructive criticism. The Bible tells us we should pursue the things which make for peace and the things by which one may edify another. Edifying one another means to encourage, build up and give support (Romans 14:19).

Let me try to put into a few words what I believe the Lord is saying to us up to this point, "Follow the rules of society and the church, unless they violate the Word of God. If you do this, you will live in peace."

Lastly, I want to address hygiene and the role that it plays in blending into society. Before we were Christians we only thought of our own needs. If we were used to living our lives outside of society's norm, we may not be used to bathing or addressing other socially accepted norms of hygiene. Does God really care about these types of things? I believe He does.

John Calvin said, "Cleanliness is next to Godliness." And Calvin was speaking a Biblical truth. God doesn't want us stinking up the place and neither does your brother. Often, our self-centeredness keeps us from doing what is best for those around us. Our pride keeps us from admitting we may have a social or hygiene problem. Concerning this issue, someone said that pride is a lot like bad breath; everybody knows you've got it but you!

I knew an elder in the church who was a wonderful brother in Christ and had much wisdom to share with those around him, but his breath was so bad, that no one wanted to be around him. It was obvious he didn't take care of his teeth. I don't think anybody had the courage to ask him to do so, but if they would have, he would have been able to minister to many more people.

In one of the recovery homes I worked in, the brothers were complaining about one of the residents who would not bathe. He was an intelligent man and a retired teacher. Besides his body odor, everyone liked him but no one could stand being around him. We eventually found out that he had had a traumatic experience involving water and was terrified to take a shower. Once this was known, several brothers would take turns being close by while he would bathe, assuring him that they would rescue him if anything should go wrong. Eventually he gained more confidence and bathed more regularly. He was much more pleasant to be around, and his ministry to the other men increased significantly.

Though you may not be offended by your own body

odors, others are. God has given us many scriptures about cleanliness. Here is just one:

> *"If one of your men is unclean because of a nocturnal emission, he is to go outside the camp and stay there. But as evening approaches he is to wash himself, and at sunset he may return to the camp. (Also), Designate a place outside the camp where you can go to relieve yourself. As part of your equipment have something to dig with, and when you relieve yourself, dig a hole and cover up your excrement. For the LORD your God moves about in your camp to protect you and to deliver your enemies to you. Your camp must be holy, so that he will not see among you anything indecent and turn away from you." (Deuteronomy 23:10-14 NIV)*

You may know the scripture in Ephesians 4:15 that says we need to speak the truth in love to each other. But remember, we need to hear the truth in love too. In other words, we need to be willing to receive correction. If we will, the Lord will speak to us through His word and the Church. The following are three scriptures in the book of Proverbs that we should all embrace if we want to become wiser men.

> *"Do not rebuke a mocker or he will hate you; rebuke a wise man and he will*

love you. Instruct a wise man and he will be wiser still; teach a righteous man and he will add to his learning." (Proverbs 9:8-9 NIV)

"Whoever loves discipline loves knowledge, but he who hates correction is stupid." (Proverbs 12:1 NIV)

"Better is open rebuke than hidden love. Wounds from a friend can be trusted, but an enemy multiplies kisses." (Proverbs 27:5-6 NIV)

In closing, I want to say that God has given us all gifts. These gifts will manifest themselves in natural and supernatural ways. We are all good at something that God wants us to use for His kingdom. However, often we never get to use these gifts to bless others because we hinder people's attempt to get close to us. The fine aroma God has given us to bless others gets overrun by the stink of personal bad habits or lack of understanding of social skills. Wise men or women understand these things and open themselves up to loving correction.

Someone once said, "Don't be porcupines; having many fine points but being impossible to get close to."

Homework

Return this list to the instructor of this class before the next lesson. If possible, also make a copy of this page for your own reference.

1. Ask one to three close friends if there is anything you can do to help them be more comfortable around you.

2. Write those suggestions down and bring them before the Lord in prayer to see what He shows you.

_____

_____

_____

_____

_____

3. After praying about the items you listed above, write down some practical things you can do to help people be more comfortable around you.

_____

_____

_____

_____

_____

<u>Notes</u>

Chapter Eight
Submission & Servanthood

"And be not drunk with wine, wherein is excess; but be filled with the Spirit; Speaking to yourselves in psalms and hymns and spiritual songs, singing and making melody in your heart to the Lord; Giving thanks always for all things unto God and the Father in the name of our Lord Jesus Christ; Submitting yourselves one to another in the fear of God." (Ephesians 5:18-21 KJV)

Submission and servanthood is one of the most important chapters in this series of teachings. It would have been great to start this book with this chapter. However, it is a little unrealistic to expect someone exiting the life of incarceration or drug addiction to grasp the revelation of this subject at the beginning of this book, or in the beginning of his or her spiritual walk.

You may remember in Chapter Four, I shared the story about a 5-year-old boy who was disciplined and told to sit in the corner for a time out. Once he assumed his position, sitting on his little stool, he looked at his mother and said, "I may be sitting down on the outside, but I'm standing up on the inside!" Most of us can relate to this little boy's reaction. We generally always want to have our own way and do our own thing.

Most people who have been incarcerated have not been raised up under good and Godly discipline. People who have had an extensive drug addiction have been led though life by their body appetites, emotions, and feelings. They have only really learned to submit to their drugs of choice.

Our flesh teaches us to serve our own needs. However, to mature in life, we need to understand the principles of Godly submission. This we will do next.

First of all, let's take a look at the word "submission."

According to Strong's Concordance, the Greek word for submission is *hupeiko* which when translated into English means: **to yield**.

On the roadways we see yield signs. They are there to keep the main flow of traffic moving and to prevent collisions with other vehicles. When we ignore these signs, we are not yielding but forcing our own way. The ultimate outcome will be an accident. The result will be chaos.

We cannot all be in charge. God established the principle of submission to keep order in our universe, and to keep order in our immediate social environment.

Below I will be listing six areas where God has displayed the principles of submission.

The first area is the Godhead, or what theologians have called the Trinity. The doctrine of the Trinity teaches us that the Father, the Son, and the Holy Spirit are all equal persons in the Godhead.

The Bible teaches us that God the Father conceived creation and presides over His creation as the heavenly judge. Jesus is described as the person through whom creation was made, and He has become the Redeemer of fallen creation. The Holy Spirit is the person who imparts to us the living truths of the Word of God.

The Bible tells us that although Jesus was equally God (Phil. 2:5-10, John 14:8-10), He has submitted all things to the Father (John 5:30). The Bible also tells us that the Holy Spirit who also is equally God, does not promote His own agenda but always points to Jesus (John 16:13-15, 1st John 2:27).

The principle of Godly submission could be illustrated then by asking three questions. First, is God the Father less God than God the Son or God the Holy Spirit? Secondly, is Jesus (God the Son), any less God than the Father or the Holy Spirit? Thirdly, is God the Holy Spirit any less God than God the Son or God the Father? The answer is obviously no. Yet each person of the Trinity submits to one another according to the will and purposes of God. Therefore, God has revealed unto us that even the Godhead exercises the principles of submission to bring order to His kingdom!

The study of the Trinity is a fascinating one. I encourage you to take some time to explore the Bible concerning it. For brevity's sake, I have listed a few of the references that support the doctrine of the Trinity in the Appendix at the back of this book. I hope these references will whet your appetite for more study. My point is this: If the principle of Godly submission is modeled in the Godhead, it must be an important principle for us in learning to walk successfully in the kingdom of God.

Secondly, God has set up order and submission *in the heavenly government* as we see in the examples given in the Bible about the activity of angels.

The Bible mentions the angelic realm had originally been created to minister unto God. The Bible reveals that its government had been set up with a rank and order in the angelic hierarchy. We are taught little about this hierarchy, but it seems archangels are the highest ranking, then perhaps seraphim and cherubim. There is a story in Daniel 10:11-13 that sheds some light on the angelic order.

One day, an angel showed up to bring Daniel an answer from God on prayers he had previously prayed. The angel told Daniel he would have arrived sooner with the answer, but certain demonic angelic princes who presided over Persia delayed him. The angel enlightened Daniel that he had to call for backup from Michael, the archangel, to clear the way for him to bring God's message to Daniel. The study of angels is another fascinating topic in the Bible. You can read more about angels and their ministry in the following scriptures— Genesis 3:24; Isaiah 6:2; Daniel 12:1; 1st Thessalonians 4:16; Hebrews 1; Jude 1:9; Revelation 12:7.

Shortly we will take a look at what the Bible describes as the first cosmic rebellion; but my point here is that God has clearly shown us that His kingdom operates on the principles of Godly submission.

Jesus asked us to pray for His Father's will to be done on earth as it is in heaven. The more you get familiar with the scriptures you will see there is a theme throughout the Bible. What happens on earth is a reflection of what is actually going on in the heavenly realm. This brings us to the third area where God wants Godly submission to take place. That place is on earth.

God has the principles of Godly submission *in our earthly government* to keep order and prevent chaos. One of the places in the Bible we see this clearly taught is in Romans 13:1-8 where we read:

> *"Let every soul be subject to the governing authorities. For there is no authority except from God, and the authorities that exist are appointed by God. Therefore whoever resists the authority resists the ordinance of God, and those who resist will bring judgment on themselves. For rulers are not a terror to good works, but to evil. Do you want to be unafraid of the authority? Do what is good, and you will have praise from the same. For he is God's minister to you for good. But if you do evil, be afraid; for he does not bear the sword in vain; for he is God's minister, an avenger to execute wrath on him who practices evil. Therefore you must be subject, not only because of wrath but also for conscience' sake. For because of this you also pay taxes, for they are God's ministers attending continually to this very thing. Render therefore to all their due: taxes to whom taxes are due, customs to whom customs, fear to whom fear, honor to whom honor.*

Owe no one anything except to love one another, for he who loves another has fulfilled the law."

Fourthly, God has set up an order of Godly submission *in the work place*. In this passage, it would be appropriate to substitute the words "bondservants" for employees and "masters" for employers. However, the principle is the same, to recognize and honor the authority over us in the work place. Ephesians 6:5-9 exhorts us:

"Bondservants, be obedient to those who are your masters according to the flesh, with fear and trembling, in sincerity of heart, as to Christ; not with eyeservice, as men-pleasers, but as bondservants of Christ, doing the will of God from the heart, with goodwill doing service, as to the Lord, and not to men, knowing that whatever good anyone does, he will receive the same from the Lord, whether he is a slave or free. And you, masters, do the same things to them, giving up threatening, knowing that your own Master also is in heaven, and there is no partiality with Him."

Fifthly, God has set up an order of Godly submission *in the family* as recorded in Ephesians 5:22-33 and Ephesians 6:1-3 where we read:

"Wives, submit to your own husbands, as to the Lord. For the husband is head of the wife, as also Christ is head of the church; and He is the Savior of the body. Therefore, just as the church is subject to Christ, so let the wives be to their own husbands in everything.

Husbands, love your wives, just as Christ also loved the church and gave Himself for her, that He might sanctify and cleanse her with the washing of water by the word, that He might present her to Himself a glorious church, not having spot or wrinkle or any such thing, but that she should be holy and without blemish. So husbands ought to love their own wives as their own bodies; he who loves his wife loves himself. For no one ever hated his own flesh, but nourishes and cherishes it, just as the Lord does the church. For we are members of His body, of His flesh and of His bones. "For this reason a man shall leave his father and mother and be joined to his wife, and the two shall become one flesh." This is a great mystery, but I speak concerning Christ and the church. Nevertheless let each one of you in particular so love his own wife as himself, and let the wife see that she respects her husband.

And, Children, obey your parents in

the Lord, for this is right. "Honor your father and mother," which is the first commandment with promise: "that it may be well with you and you may live long on the earth." And you, fathers, do not provoke your children to wrath, but bring them up in the training and admonition of the Lord."

Lastly, God has set up an order of Godly submission *in the Church*—Ephesians 5:17-21 where the Apostle Paul writes:

"Therefore do not be unwise, but understand what the will of the Lord is. And do not be drunk with wine, in which is dissipation; but be filled with the Spirit, speaking to one another in psalms and hymns and spiritual songs, singing and making melody in your heart to the Lord, giving thanks always for all things to God the Father in the name of our Lord Jesus Christ, submitting to one another in the fear of God."

Satan gave us our first view of rebellion against God's principles of submission. We read in the Bible that Satan was one of God's highest creations in the angelic realm, perhaps even an archangel (Ezekiel 28:13-19), but that was not good enough for him. Satan wanted to occupy a position he was not created for. His pride and lust for power caused him to rebel against God. You may want to take time to read about this in Isaiah 14:12-15. This passage of scripture has become well known as the *"Five I wills of Satan."* We are reminded here to guard our hearts against pride and discontent.

Revelation 12:4 tells us that Satan was cast down out of heaven, along with a third of the angels. Most theologians believe this was the first cosmic rebellion. It might not have taken long after this for Satan to approach God's creation here on earth, to tempt them to rebel against God also. We read in Genesis 2:16-17 that God told Adam and Eve they could eat of any tree in the garden except from the Tree of Knowledge. Satan, however, tempted Eve to rebel against God by convincing her that God was holding out on something special. He convinced her to doubt God's word, doubt God's love, and doubt God's protection for her. In Eve's naiveté, she partook of the forbidden fruit and convinced her husband to do the same (Genesis 3:1-6). This event caused mankind to enter into sin. Ever since that act of rebellion, man began to develop a mindset of lawlessness. We too have inherited this same sinful character trait of rebellion that Satan demonstrated against God's authority (and really, all authority).

The consequences of rebellion have been dramatically illustrated throughout the Bible. One of the places where rebellion and its negative consequences are demonstrated is in the life of King Saul. You may want to read the story for yourself, but basically Saul (like Adam and Eve) was given a kingdom. Yet, Saul (like Adam and Eve) could not accept the authority over him.

Ultimately, he lost all his authority. Read with me in 1st Samuel 15:23 where Saul is reproved by Samuel the prophet after many opportunities to get his act together:

> *"For rebellion is as the sin of witchcraft, and stubbornness is as iniquity and idolatry. Because you have rejected the word of the LORD, He also has rejected you from being king."*

I have listed several negative results from not understanding or not practicing the principles of Godly submission. Now I would like to list some of the positive results of Godly submission. First, Godly submission brings wisdom and prevents heartache for those who practice it. We read in Hebrews that God will be faithful to bring spiritual mentors into our lives to help us mature in our Christian walk.

We are encouraged in Hebrews 13:17 to:

> *"Obey them that have the rule over you, and submit yourselves: for they watch for your souls, as they that must give account, that they may do it with joy, and not with grief: for that is unprofitable for you."* (ASV)

Learning to submit in a Godly manner corrects our critical spirit and teaches us to be content. A person who is maturing in their faith is a person who accepts Godly correction. Proverbs 9:7-9 tells us:

"Whoever corrects a mocker invites insult; whoever rebukes a wicked man incurs abuse. Do not rebuke a mocker or he will hate you; rebuke a wise man and he will love you. Instruct a wise man and he will be wiser still; teach a righteous man and he will add to his learning."

We are wise to listen to those who have more experience than we do. We are even wiser, if we take their advice.

Jesus said in John 13:16-17:

"Most assuredly, I say to you, a servant is not greater than his master nor is he who is sent greater than he who sent him. If you know these things, blessed are you if you do them." (See also James 1:22-25)

In other words, we don't just listen to what Jesus says; we also need to **do** what He says.

In Chapter Four I shared that it is our responsibility to find Godly leadership to help us grow in Christ. This may be hard for us because we struggle with authority and may have been hurt by authority in the past. But know this: good leadership realizes that God is holding them accountable to shepherd the flock of God with integrity. James 3:1 states that:

"My brethren, let not many of you

become teachers, knowing that we shall receive a stricter judgment."

Another benefit of applying the principles of Godly submission is that it forces us to work with one another. Although younger Christians are exhorted to submit or yield to their elders, no one is exempt from learning Godly submission. 1st Peter 5:5-6 tells us:

"Likewise you younger people, submit yourselves to your elders. Yes, all of you be submissive to one another, and be clothed with humility, for "God resists the proud, But gives grace to the humble." Therefore humble yourselves under the mighty hand of God, that He may exalt you in due time."

We read in this passage that submission is not a one-way street.

The Lord will constantly be bringing people into our lives that have ideas contrary to ours, to teach us how to work with one another. Sometimes these brothers and sisters will be older or younger than us. They may be of the opposite gender. They may be of a different culture or financial status. Through these people who think differently than us, God will reveal that our opinion or way is not always the best or right way, when it comes to the kingdom of God.

I can remember a time when this was especially true in my life. I was taking classes at a local junior college with our youth pastor, to try to evangelize on the college campus. Our church was renting Sunday space for our worship service in the Science Lab at this college, and to us it made sense that we should be reaching out to the students.

Our youth pastor and I chose a couple of classes to validate our attendance and give us access to student body resources. I was probably one of the oldest, if not the oldest, student at this college. We worked alongside the young Christian students who were trying to start a Bible club. Before we had arrived, they were unable to meet the attendance requirements of 10 registered students. With our presence and ministry gifting, we were able to help them become a viable Christian outreach on campus. One young lady, who was much different than I was in personality and spiritual expression, was a key leader in the group. She liked to talk, and she always had ideas that she wanted to share with the group. Since we (myself and the youth pastor) were men, in full-time ministry, and also seemed to be the club rescuers, we felt we always had the definitive word for direction for the club. However, I lost count of how many times the Lord revealed His will through this sister, to show me I was just stubborn and presumptuous.

One day, we were trying to find a different place to have a Christian concert on the campus instead of the noisy cafeteria where we usually had them. I had an idea for a particular place. She was against the place I had in mind. I argued that I knew what made good sense when it came to this type of outreach. She pleaded with me to follow her to a different place for the venue. I was adamant that I knew the right place the Lord wanted the concert. Although I argued my plan, I could hear the still small voice of the Lord telling me to listen to her. He used this young lady to lead us to a beautiful recital hall with plush red seating, carpeted stage, and gorgeous curtains hanging high above the platform. It was perfect, and I didn't even know that it existed.

Ultimately, I pursued the college to rent us this room for our Sunday worship services. They were happy to do so for the same price we were paying for the Science Lab, which really was a dismal room for a church service—there was no real atmosphere to enhance worship. The only intriguing decoration in the room was a science table in front for dissecting frogs and other scientific experiments. The table, with a Bunsen burner intact, became our communion table and altar. I must admit the Bunsen burner made for great illustrations on the fires of hell during a sermon. Oh, how I would have missed this opportunity to find a better place to have Sunday worship services if we had followed my plan.

Submitting to one another is part of fulfilling the revelation of the servanthood of Christ. Christ demonstrated the importance of embracing serving—to teach us humility. He set the example and encourages us to follow in His footsteps.

Paul wrote in Philippians 2:3-8:

> *"Let nothing be done through strife or vainglory; but in lowliness of mind let each esteem others better than themselves. Look not every man on his own things, but every man also on the things of others. Let this*

mind be in you, which was also in Christ Jesus: Who, being in the form of God, thought it not robbery to be equal with God: But made Himself of no reputation, and took upon Him the form of a servant, and was made in the likeness of men: And being found in fashion as a man, He humbled Himself, and became obedient unto death, even the death of the cross."

We are to follow in Christ's footsteps, believing where He is leading us is the best way to learn how to follow God and love our fellow man. We are not to be doormats, but we are to be stepping-stones. We yield to each other to see God's work get done in God's way.

Lastly, the testimony of Godly submission brings conviction to the world. Remember, we have rebellion bred into us. The Church is to act differently than the world when it comes to submission and authority. God intends for the church to be a testimony of the benefits of trusting a loving God.

Paul writes in 1st Peter 2:13-17:

"Therefore submit yourselves to every ordinance of man for the Lord's sake, whether to the king as supreme, or to governors, as to those who are sent by Him for the punishment of evildoers and for the praise of those who do good. For this is the will of God, that by doing good you may put to silence the ignorance of foolish men—as

free, yet not using liberty as a cloak for vice, but as bondservants of God. Honor all people. Love the brotherhood. Fear God. Honor the king."

The goal of all the teaching in this chapter is to bring us to a place of spiritual wholeness, that we may be used for God's purposes in ministry. The word ministry simply means, **"to serve."** You may for the first time in your life want to enter into full-time ministry. Many people think the highest position in the church is the pastor's position. This surely is a good vocation to pursue if you are called to it; but remember, Jesus said if we wanted to be great in the kingdom of God we must become the *"servants of all."*

The first principle to learning how to be a minister is just simply learning how to be a servant. Paul, the writer of most of the New Testament, and one of the most admired men in the Bible, started his epistle to the Romans by writing:

"Paul, a servant of Jesus Christ, called to be an apostle, separated unto the gospel of God."

Being a servant of Jesus Christ is for all of us. It is a general calling of God. Being an apostle is a specific calling of God. The Holy Spirit of God is telling us in the passage above that we must be willing to fulfill the general calling of God before a specific calling will be presented to us by the Lord.

What do you think?

Homework

Return this homework assignment to the instructor of this class before the next lesson. If possible, also make a copy of this page for your own reference.

1. Over the next week, spend some time in prayer before the Lord. Ask Him to reveal situations or authority figures in your life that you have struggled with concerning submission. (These situations should be ones that you now realize that God had placed you in to teach you something). Briefly write these experiences down.

_____

_____

_____

_____

2. Pray and ask the Lord to reveal how you should have acted differently in each case. Briefly write down how you should have reacted and the possible results if you would have reacted differently.

_____

_____

_____

_____

3. Write some reminder tips on what you can do in the future to help you respond in the correct manner.

_____

_____

_____

_____

_____

_____

_____

_____

_____

_____

_____

_____

_____

_____

_____

The Testimony of Art Lyons
<u>Salvation</u>

I was born prematurely in 1953, with a double hernia. The hernia developed into serious complications, and I almost died. I was told I was a sickly child, and I became a hypochondriac.

I grew up in several broken homes. My mother was married three times before she was 28, so I had one biological father and two stepfathers before I was in the 2nd grade. My mother divorced my father when I was three. Alcoholism was prevalent on both sides of my family. My mother died of cirrhosis of the liver when she was only 41.

My sister and I spent most of our time with our grandparents. My grandmother was a cheerleader for me, and my grandfather was my mentor; they instilled many good values in me. I always attended Sunday School when I stayed with them. This spiritual influence established my faith in Jesus. I believed there was a God and Jesus was His Son, but I did not understand more than that. When I would pray as a child, He brought me comfort from many fears and insecurities.

When I was in the 1st grade, my mother married her fourth husband. He was a medical assistant in the Navy. He wanted me to be a tough kid and fight back when I was picked on, but this was against my nature. He also talked about medical diseases that added to my fears. We moved a lot, and at each school I was picked on. In the

5th grade, I discovered that if I would be willing to fight back and hang out with the toughest kids in the school, I would be left alone. This lifestyle began a pattern for me for the next 10 years.

In junior high, I started to smoke cigarettes and experiment with drugs and alcohol. When I was 15, I had a bad trip on LSD and experienced flashbacks and depression. By age 16, alcohol seemed to give me the feeling of security, and I relied on alcohol as my way to deal with life's pressures. It also masked some of the psychological problems that developed from the bad LSD trip. For the next three years, I abused alcohol or drugs every day.

During high school, my friend Bob (who used to do psychedelic drugs) became a Christian. He had an inner peace in his life that affected me deeply. I wanted to have this peace but did not know how to get it. I attended some meetings at his church and tried to give my life over to the Lord, but my enthusiasm didn't last. After that, I went back to my old lifestyle for five years.

Between the ages of 15 and 21, I was arrested several times for crimes, and I spent some time in jail. By the time I was 19, I was smoking 2-3 packs of cigarettes a day and drinking heavily. I also was having back pain from a work-related injury that caused me great discomfort and anxiety. I drank more heavily in an attempt to mask how I felt emotionally and physically.

Eventually, I became concerned about smoking because I had pain in my chest and left arm. Because of my Lutheran background, I said the "Lord's Prayer" every night before I passed out from drinking. One night,

I asked God to help me quit smoking any way He could. Suddenly, I became afraid and wondered if God would give me cancer. Several days later, a friend told me her father had died of lung cancer. The description of his ailments was close to how I was feeling, so I thought I was developing cancer too. This "healthy fear" motivated me to stop smoking. This was my first experience in seeing God answer prayer in a mysterious, powerful way in my adult life.

After I overcame my cigarette addiction, my lifestyle of drinking and fighting every night began to wear me out. There were some people trying to hurt me, including some members of the Hell's Angels Motorcycle Club. As the days rolled by, I became fearful and depressed and started wondering if life was worth living. Yet, at the same time, I was terribly frightened of dying. On top of all this, I had a friend who said he was a warlock. He told me that I was going to die when I was 21. I tried not to pay any attention to him, but when I thought more about it I began to experience extreme paranoia.

As my paranoia increased, I thought I was going to die, and saw everyone as a threat. I became so anxious I could not sleep or eat, unless I was thoroughly drunk. At the same time, I took note of a young man named David, the youngest brother of a friend. He lived at a major party house where I frequently drank. He had given his life to Christ, and I could tell that he had the same inner peace in his life that my friend Bob had in high school. Again, I was drawn to wanting to know how to have this experience, but I couldn't understand what to do to get it.

I thought that if I died I would go to hell, so I wondered how I could prove to God I was serious about wanting change in my life. In March of 1975, I sought the Lord for deliverance from my fears of physical death and eternal hell fire.

In 1975, my friends and I decided to go camping. I played music and sought a spiritual experience. However, I did not seem to find comfort. Back at home, I ended up drinking with a buddy while watching Cecil B. DeMille's movie "The Ten Commandments" on TV. When the movie got to the part of Moses parting the Red Sea, I prayed in my mind to the Lord that I believed He really did perform those miracles in Egypt. I told the Lord I was very unhappy with my life, and that I needed a miracle of deliverance from all the stuff that was robbing me of my peace of mind.

Suddenly, three questions from the Lord came into my mind. The first one was, "Why don't you become a Christian?" and I responded, "Because I would be bored as a Christian." To me, Christians could not wear hippy-style clothing, could not listen to rock and roll, and could not ride motorcycles, all the things that were important to me.

The second question was, "Yes, but what if becoming a Christian would make you happy?" I responded, "Well, if becoming a Christian would bring me happiness, I would go for it, but I don't think I could be happy as a Christian."

Then, a third time the same type of question was asked of me, "Yes, but if becoming a Christian truly would bring you happiness, isn't this what you want?" I responded, "Yes, Lord. I don't understand how becoming a Christian would bring me happiness, but if this is true, then I will give my life to you." I added, "But you'll have to do a miracle, because I don't see how it could work." After saying those words, I knew something had changed in me, but was not sure what. I turned to my drinking buddy and told him that I would be going to church the next day.

That evening, as always, I was severely anxious. But when I thought about sharing God with people, I felt a deep, inner peace. When I thought about my problems, I became fearful. I tried to keep my mind on what little I knew of God, so I could experience peace. I felt my life was going to be different somehow.

The following week—something miraculous happened—I had no desire for alcohol. Previous to my encounter with God, I could not have abstained from drinking for a single day. There were supernatural changes in my life, but I was still struggling with my fears of death and hell. So I tried to convince God of my sincerity.

The following Sunday, I went to the church my friend David attended. I was absorbing what the preacher was saying like a sponge absorbs water. When he finished his sermon, he invited people to the altar for prayer, if they wanted to show God they were serious about their relationship with Him. That created a dilemma in me.

My prayer all week was, "What could I do to show God I was serious?" but I also was too proud to parade myself in front of people, acknowledging that I was a sinner. I struggled with the decision, but at the same time I felt compelled to go to the altar for prayer. Before I knew what happened, I was at the altar weeping, and I felt a giant burden of guilt, shame, and sin lift off of me. Then the peace of God came flooding in. I knew that I was in Christ and He was in me. I knew this was the place that I needed to be for the rest of my life.

Call to Ministry

Although our testimonies never really end, that was my first week's experience in the Lord, and my salvation experience. Within the next days and months, I realized that God was healing me from many fears and insecurities developed from my childhood.

Shortly after my conversion, there was a desire in me to be a minister. It was difficult to really believe that God would use me in this way, but He encouraged me in this direction. I seemed to grow fast spiritually. I liked spending lots of time with people who were in ministry. I helped them in what they were doing as much as I was able and would lead worship and Bible studies whenever they asked me.

Four years after my conversion, I asked the leadership at the church I was attending what I should do to be trained for full-time ministry. They said I should go to Bible school and suggested one affiliated with the church. I started that year.

In Bible school, we were introduced to leaders of various ministries. These leaders would share exciting testimonies of God's guidance and provision in their lives. We were challenged to make a commitment of internship for a full year to one of these ministries after graduation. I was really looking forward to which ministry the Lord would call me. I had several in mind as the Bible school progressed.

One of the leaders who came and shared was in charge of a prison ministry. Of all the ministries for which I felt no desire, prison and hospital ministry was at the top of my list. Hospitals made me feel uneasy because as a child I was fearful of diseases. I can't really say why the prison ministry bothered me. Perhaps it was because of my background with drugs and alcohol. I knew all too well the games my old buddies played. Or perhaps I felt uncomfortable because just recently, the pastor of the church I was attending had asked me to disciple a brother in Christ who had just gotten out of prison.

I had spent quite a significant amount of time finding this ex-convict a place to live with another brother who was stable in the Lord. I also had introduced him to a new brother in Christ who was trying to break ties with the Hell's Angels Motorcycle Club. I thought introducing them all to each other would be good fellowship for them. Three weeks later, the brother fresh out of prison violated his parole and was re-arrested. The ex-biker had disappeared, and the brother who was just trying to help out was now left with unaffordable rent payments on a three-bedroom house. Everything that could have gone wrong did go wrong.

Now, getting back to this prison minister's

presentation, when we took a break to stretch, I did not even want to talk to this minister. However, out of respect and politeness, I decided to strike up a conversation with him. I discovered that he knew the ex-con brother with whom I'd been assigned to work, and he was currently visiting him in jail. He also invited me to meet with him later to talk more about prison ministry. I respectfully declined his offer. But I felt a little like Jonah refusing to preach to the Ninevites.

During the next several months, I would see this prison minister from time to time around the school campus. He would always invite me to meet with him, but I always found a way to avoid making an appointment.

After graduating from Bible school, I began seeking the Lord for the ministry He was calling me to. I volunteered for a couple of different ministries but did not feel any long-term desire for them. After a few months, I really felt urgency in my spirit that it was time to find a ministry in which to be committed but all the doors of ministry seemed to be shut for me. As I was diligently seeking the Lord for direction, once again, I crossed paths with the prison minister. Once again, he invited me to meet with him. I finally agreed to, and so we set up a meeting.

I was to meet him at his office at 9 am on a Monday morning. So Monday, I was waiting for him outside his office at 9 am sharp, but he did not show up. As I tried to wait patiently, I became more and more frustrated; in particular, frustrated over the fact that I did not want to be involved in prison ministry. Furthermore, this guy who kept bugging me, *NOW* doesn't even show up.

After waiting for a half an hour, I came to the conclusion that if he wanted me to work with him, he would have to meet **all** of my requirements. This is not exactly how they taught us in Bible school to approach ministry opportunities. We were taught to humbly yield ourselves as servants. We were supposed to be willing to do anything that was available for us. We were told that in God's time, He would raise us up to the ministry we were called to.

Around 9:30 am, when I was about to leave, I saw a fellow Bible student walking by who asked me what I was doing standing all alone. I explained I was waiting to meet with the prison minister. He told me that in the morning all the pastors met in a different office for devotions, and he directed me to where he was. After I finally found the prison minister, he asked me what it would take for me to work with him. I thought to myself, *this is my opportunity to let him know of everything **I** expected of him*. I felt that he would probably want to avoid such a prideful intern, and I could be off to look for a better ministry to commit to. He listened to my conditions and then said ok to all of them.

What could I do? I could not find an excuse not to work with him. So, that morning I began working with him; and during the next few months, the Lord just exploded the ministry. He opened up to us more opportunities than we were able to handle.

That was almost thirty years ago. Many things have changed since then, but the Lord has always opened doors for me concerning correctional ministry. As I have shared, I did not start out with a passion for this type of ministry. I did however have a passion to minister the Gospel. In my personal experience, I have come to believe that if we want to minister the Gospel, God will give us the desire of our hearts. Yet, the ministry He has for us is not always where or how we expect it to be. I often think of Paul the Apostle and how his heart's desire was to minister to his Jewish brethren, but God called him to be the Apostle to the Gentiles.

To further illustrate this point, I can remember talking to a fellow Chaplain (a very good friend) back in 1985. We were the Facility Chaplains for a Detention Facility in Chula Vista, California. During our conversation, we were reminiscing on how God had guided us to work together in this jail. He told me that after he accepted Christ, he felt a calling to the ministry, but he asked the Lord not to send him to the hospitals or the jails to minister. I shared the same thing, and we both burst out laughing at the Lord's sense of humor.

What is He doing in your life?

Art Lyons Biography

Art Lyons felt called to the ministry, after his conversion at the age of 20, which saved him from a life of drug abuse, alcoholism, and periodic jail time. Five years later, in 1980, he graduated from the Horizon School of Evangelism (HSE), majoring in counseling, and he has been in some type of full-time ministry (volunteer and professional) ever since. He currently divides his time between ministry in his local church and jail ministry. In his 30 years in the ministry, Art has been ordained and licensed with the following churches: Calvary Chapel, Cornerstone Christian Community, and Christian & Missionary Alliance, all in Chula Vista, California.

Although Art will admit he did not start out with a desire to work for the Lord in the correctional ministry, God has always opened doors for him there. Art served as a Chaplain with the San Diego Sheriff's Department for 17 years and has assisted in developing policies and procedures that govern the ministry of Chaplains in many correctional institutions in San Diego.

From 1980 to 1999, Art was an active member of the San Diego County Jail Ministries (SDCJM) and served on the Board as Director of Services, from 1997 through 1999. Also during that time, Art held a position on the Executive Board of the Most Excellent Way (TMEW), to offer his input and leadership skills regarding starting a recovery home and to be an advisor for re-entry resources.

Art is founder and director of the non-profit organization, **Re-Entry Prison and Jail Ministry** (RPJM). RPJM provides for after-care in the San Diego area. He annually produces a San Diego Re-Entry Resource Directory and maintains a San Diego specific website that offers re-entry information and correctional ministry educational materials.

From 2000 to 2008, Art trained and mentored new chaplains giving them the necessary skills to have an effective ministry inside and outside of correctional facilities in San Diego County.

Art has completed the Institute of Chaplaincy Studies at Vision International University (VIU), and has earned a Master's degree in Theological Studies & Counseling from VIU and is currently working on his Doctorate of Ministry.

Before Christ   **After Christ**

Contact information:

Re-Entry Prison and Jail Ministry
Pastor Art Lyons
PO Box 620
Chula Vista, CA 91912

Phone: (619) 482-7258

Email: reentry@reentry.org
Website: www.reentry.org

Appendix

There are many Bible passages that reveal the teaching of the Trinity of God, but I will just mention a few here. Keep in mind that the revelation of doctrine in the Bible is progressive. What this means is that as time progressed from creation to the time of Christ, so did God reveal more about Himself to mankind.

In the Old Testament:

Isaiah 42:1—*"Behold! My Servant whom I uphold, My Elect One in whom My soul delights! I have put My Spirit upon Him; He will bring forth justice to the Gentiles.* Notice the three Persons in this first example. The first Person is the Speaker, who is identified by the pronoun I. The second Person is the Speaker's servant, the Servant of Jehovah. And the third person is the Spirit of God.

Isaiah 61:1— *"The Spirit of the Lord GOD is upon Me, because the LORD has anointed Me to preach good tidings to the poor; He has sent Me to heal the brokenhearted, to proclaim liberty to the captives, and the opening of the prison to those who are bound;* ... This example mentions three individuals; the Lord Jehovah; the Spirit of Jehovah; and the pronoun me, in reference to the Speaker: The Spirit of the Lord Jehovah is upon me in the reference to Christ.

In the New Testament:

Matthew 3:16-17 — *"When He had been baptized, Jesus came up immediately from the water; and behold, the heavens were opened to Him, and He saw the Spirit* *of God descending like a dove and alighting upon Him. And suddenly a voice came from heaven, saying, "This is My beloved Son, in whom I am well pleased."* The Son is seen in the Person of Jesus; the Spirit is seen because He comes down in the bodily form of a dove; and the Father is made present by the audible voice that comes down out of the heavens, saying: *"This is my beloved Son, in whom I am well pleased."*

Matthew 28:19—*"Go ye therefore, and make disciples of all the nations, baptizing them into the name of the Father and the Son and the Holy Spirit:"* In the second example of the Trinity of the Godhead in the New Testament, these three Persons are now given titles of Father, Son, and Holy Spirit. Notice the seeming contradiction insofar as the grammar is concerned. The command is to go and baptize in the **name** of, and the word name is singular in the original language. It does not say, "in the names of the Father, Son and Holy Spirit," which would have been more grammatically correct. But rather, it is in the name of. The word name is singular, emphasizing the unity of the Godhead. This one name belongs to the Father, the Son, and the Holy Spirit, emphasizing the Trinity of the Godhead.

John 14:16-17—*And I will pray to the Father, and He will give you another Helper, that He may abide with you forever—the Spirit of truth, whom the world cannot receive, because it neither sees Him nor knows Him; but you know Him, for He dwells with you and will be in you.* In the third example of the Trinity of the Godhead in the New Testament, notice again the three Persons mentioned in this context. One Person is the Speaker,

Jesus, who is identified by the pronoun I. The second Person is the Father to whom He will pray. The third Person is the [Holy] Spirit, who is going to be sent.[1]

---

[1] My thanks to Arnold Fruchtenbaum and Arial Ministries for permission to use the illustrations regarding the Trinity. For a complete copy of this study go to: http://www.arielm.org/dcs/pdf/mbs050m.pdf.

Notes

www.ingramcontent.com/pod-product-compliance
Lightning Source LLC
LaVergne TN
LVHW021507080426
835509LV00018B/2430